CW01663576

Cabral
Alburquerque
Rua Tap Siac
Restoration Row
Avenida do Conselheiro Ferreira de Almeida
Rua Ferreira do Amaral
Estrada da Vitoria
St. Michael Cemetery
Estrada do Cemiterio
Rua Eduardo Marques
St. Lazarus Church
Vasco da Gama Monument
Rua de Joao de Almeida
Calcada Igreja de S. Lazaro
Rua Nova de S. Lazaro
Rua do Volong
Calcada Central de S. Lazaro
Rua S. Miguel
Rua S. Roque
Calcada Poco
T. Santos
T. Do Pato
Calcada do Gaio
Estrada do Engenheiro
Estrada de Cacilhas
Parsee Cemetery
Colina do Visconde De S. Januario
Estrada Visconde de S. Januario
Rua Nova a Guia
Estrada S. Francisco
Government Hospital
Avenida do Dr. Rodrigo Rodrigues
St. Raphael Hospital
Calcada Monte
Rua Pedro Nolasco da Silva
Rua do Campo
Rua Noronha
Restaurant Portugues
Teatro Diocesano
Travessa dos Anjos
S. Domingos
St. Francis Gardens
Calcada dos Quarteis
St. Francis Barracks
Rua Santa Clara
Avenida Amizade
Macau Cathedral
Largo da Se
Military Club
Rua da Se
T. Praia Grande
Rua Comandante Mata E. Oliveira
Jose Lobo
Avenida d. Joao IV
Avenida de Lopo Sarmento de Carvalho
Lisboa Hotel and Casino
Praia Grande
Avenida Infante D. Henrique
Rua Dr. Pedro
Bank of China Building
Avenida Amizade
Rua da Praia
Ferreira do Amaral Monument
Baia da Praia Grande
Macau - Taipa Bridge

Macau and Environs

400 km / 249 miles

INSIGHT POCKET GUIDES

Macau

Written and Presented by **Joseph R. Yogerst**

INSIGHT POCKET GUIDES

Insight Pocket Guide:

Macau

Directed by
Hans Höfer

Managing Editor
Francis Dorai

Photography by
Joseph R Yogerst and others

Design Concept by
V. Barl

Design by
Laddawan Wong

© **1994 APA Publications (HK) Ltd**

All Rights Reserved

Printed in Singapore by
Höfer Press (Pte) Ltd
Fax: 65-8616438

Distributed in the UK & Ireland by
GeoCenter International UK Ltd
The Viables Center, Harrow Way
Basingstoke, Hampshire RG22 4BJ
ISBN: 9-62421-560-X

Worldwide distribution enquiries:
Höfer Communications Pte Ltd
38 Joo Koon Road
Singapore 2262
ISBN: 9-62421-560-X

NO part of this book may be reproduced, stored in a retrieval system or transmitted in any form or means electronic, mechanical, photocopying, recording or otherwise, without prior written permission of Apa Publications. Brief text quotations with use of photographs are exempted for book review purposes only.
As every effort is made to provide accurate information in this publication, we would appreciate it if readers would call our attention to any errors that may occur by communicating with Apa Villa, 81 The Cut, London SE1 8LL. Tel: 71-620-0008, Fax: 71-620-1074.
Information has been obtained from sources believed to be reliable, but its accuracy and completeness, and the opinions based thereon, are not guaranteed.

Bem-vindo!

Joseph R Yogerst

I first went to Macau in the mid-1980s to attend a boisterous affair called the Last China Ball at the Bela Vista Hotel. The event was meant to mark a transition between the sleepy and somewhat backward Macau to a new and dynamic Macau that was meant to emerge by the end of the 1980s. And as if our ball wasn't enough to mark the change, the first McDonald's restaurant in the colony opened that very same weekend.

I think most of us scoffed at the notion of Macau becoming brash and bold like nearby Hong Kong. You just couldn't picture it 10 years ago. Surely the paint would always be peeling off the walls of the old Portuguese villas along the Praia Grande and there would always be a green swath of rice paddies across the middle of Taipa Island. I was wrong.

Macau has changed beyond my wildest expectations. The villas are still there along the Praia Grande, but they must compete for space with new office towers like the Bank of China Building, one of the highest in Asia. Taipa's rice paddies have since given way to modern condo blocks and apartments, but the village is still there, as lively and as exciting as ever. My itineraries are designed to capture the spirit of this colony that blends European charm and the exotic East so comfortably. Whether you've opted for a full-day tour of the Praia Grande and old city, an afternoon sussing out bargains in the Tercena district with its dark and moody lanes, or an evening of revelry at one of the city's many casinos and cabarets, you'll be held in awe.

What I like most about Macau is that you can still find slices of the past that have survived intact. And that's what this book is all about: revealing to you the parts of Macau that retain their bygone splendour and charm. *Bem-Vindo — Welcome!*

AIRSPEED
MPH
20
40
60
80
100
120
140

Contents

Preceding pages: Macau from the open cockpit of an Ultralite plane

---

Maps

Following pages: facade of St Paul's Church

SIGNA

History

Statue of Vasco da Gama

Macau is one of the great accidents of Asian history. It should never have existed in the first place – at least not as a Portuguese colony – and it is something of a miracle that it has endured for so long.

The Portuguese Sail to China

Vasco da Gama laid the groundwork for the establishment of Macau when he sailed around the Cape of Good Hope in 1498 on a voyage of discovery that eventually took him to India. In one bold stroke, da Gama succeeded where Christopher Columbus had failed: he found a new path between Europe and the Orient that bypassed the long caravan routes through Central Asia.

After capturing the Malayan port city of Malacca, the Portuguese despatched their first expedition to Cathay in 1513. Although rebuffed by Chinese officials, Admiral Jorge Alvares returned to Malacca with word that Marco Polo's fabled land did indeed exist – and that it was as rich as the Venetian had claimed.

It took the Portuguese another five years to gain an audience with the Dragon Throne in Peking, a less than auspicious occasion at which the Chinese emperor announced to Portuguese envoy Tome Pires that he did not know where or what Portugal was. Meanwhile, unknown to Pires, his comrades launched an unsuccessful naval assault on Canton. Pires was arrested by Chinese officials and died in captivity.

This did little to stop the Portuguese, who were bound and determined to open direct trade with China. They established their first beachhead on the Chinese coast in 1540, at a place called Liampo near present-day Shanghai – a rustic settlement that Portuguese mapmakers soon labelled the 'first European settlement in

Culture

China' – and that is where they probably would have stayed if the Dragon Throne had let them. Blown off-course on a voyage to Liampo, Portuguese explorer Fernao Mendes Pinto discovered Japan and people who were more than willing to trade with the Portuguese. Liampo flourished for nearly a decade as a staging point for the Japan trade, until 1549 when Chinese troops overran the settlement.

The Portuguese traders retreated and regrouped at Sanchuang island, about 80km (50 miles) from present-day Macau. Far from the seat of imperial power in Peking, they were able to establish a thriving black market trade along the coast of southern China. Meanwhile, St Francis Xavier died at Sanchuang in 1552 after failing to convert China to Christianity. Shortly after, the Portuguese moved their trading post again, to Lampakkau island near the mouth of the Pearl River.

The four winds blow hard and steady for Portuguese explorers in this 1519 map

A Portuguese carrack

A Gift from China

Not far from Lampakkau was Macau, an unimportant narrow peninsula with a small fishing village. In 1557, it was ceded to the Portuguese as a gift for banishing pirates from the Pearl River Delta. At the same time, the Portuguese were also awarded a monopoly on Canton exports.

Macau prospered over the next 80 years as the major hub for trade in the Far East. Portuguese carracks choked the harbour, their holds laden with Japanese silver, East Indian spices, Chinese silk, tea and porcelain. It was said to rival Venice in the wealth of its trade. The old fishing village gave way to a bustling city of 6,000 people with stone warehouses, villas and Catholic churches on nearly every street – a Chinese version of Portugal.

By the early 17th century, the Dutch had established their foothold in the Orient, on the island of Java. One of their goals was to loosen Portuguese control of the China trade. To do this, they attacked Macau several times. The most celebrated episode was in June 1627 – the feast day of St John the Baptist – when they caught Macau without a full complement of soldiers. Led by Jesuit priests and black African slaves, the Macanese tried to hold the city against overwhelming odds. They were on the verge of defeat when a lucky cannon shot fired by a Jesuit priest scored a direct hit on the Dutch flagship, igniting the powder magazine in a spectacular explosion that sent the Dutch fleeing.

The Qing Emperor Kangxi

Another challenge appeared along the coast in 1637: the arrival of an English fleet which attacked Chinese troops in the Pearl River Delta before being driven away. Searching for a scapegoat, the mandarins in Canton blamed the Macanese for allowing the 'red beards' to infiltrate so far upriver and revoked Portuguese trade rights. Two years later, the Japanese shogun terminated foreign trade and executed all Christian converts. In 1641, the Dutch took Malacca. The colony fell into economic gloom as the Portuguese commercial empire in East Asia vanished almost overnight. The Golden Age of Macau was over.

The Transitional Period

Trade in Canton resumed in 1685 at the behest of Emperor Kangxi, but on a more limited basis with no single European nation granted a monopoly. Macau enjoyed a reversal of fortunes, but it was nothing like the Golden Age. China's export policy changed again in 1757, after the emperor granted the Canton merchants' guild exclusive rights to all foreign trade. The merchants in turn made life rough for the European traders, prohibiting their residence in Canton between March and September, and demanding stiff kickbacks. As a result, the traders spent spring and summer in Macau, transforming it into a cosmopolitan community of Portuguese, Dutch, English, French and American traders.

Napoleon was to blame for the next hiccup in Macau's long and tumultuous history. After France invaded Portugal in 1802, the British moved to snatch the new overseas possessions of their longtime rival. A British fleet was despatched from India with orders to capture Macau, but the Treaty of Amiens was signed before the ships reached their destination.

Two years later, Napoleon invaded Austria and once again the British pounced on the overseas possessions of French allies. They snatched the Cape of Good Hope and Ceylon from the Dutch, and Goa and Macau from the Portuguese. But the British completely underestimated the Chinese response to their actions in the Orient. A Chinese army marched across the border and trade ground to a halt until the Macanese merchants persuaded the British forces to withdraw. Chinese forces occupied Macau for a brief spell until the situation stabilised.

Weary of using Macau as their primary trading post in the Far East, the British moved to establish their own port in 1841. After

Early British sketches of Chinese merchants

CHINESE MERCHANTS, &c.

1 in their Summer Dress..... 2 in the Winter Dress..... 3 a Merchant's Wife.....

In 1841, the British negotiated and enforced the opening of Chinese ports to trade

negotiations with the Chinese broke down, Captain Charles Elliot of the Royal Navy attacked and occupied Canton. Three days later, the mandarins agreed to cede Hong Kong, a barren island on the opposite side of the Pearl River Delta from Macau. The British planted the Union Jack on January 26, but no one could have guessed at the time that Hong Kong would soon surpass Macau as the chief port on the China coast.

In 1845, the Lisbon government decided to release Macau from the direct control of colonial administrators in Goa. In doing so, they established a new province which included Timor and Solor in the Indonesian archipelago. In another policy shift, Macanese authorities refused to pay the colony's annual tribute to the Dragon Throne. Weakened by internal chaos, China did not have the power to collect its 'rent'.

That same year, an international incident transpired after a British Protestant missionary refused to remove his hat during a Corpus Christi procession through the streets of Macau. He was arrested and thrown in jail. Hong Kong responded by despatching a contingent of Royal Marines, who killed a Portuguese soldier during a successful attempt to free the missionary. Civil strife resumed four years later when the governor of Macau was assassinated by rebellious Cantonese residents. Order was not restored until Portuguese forces blew up a Chinese border post.

A Formal Treaty is Signed

After more than 400 years without a formal agreement on Macau, the Portuguese and Chinese finally inked a treaty in 1862 that bestowed on the Portuguese a colonial status similar to that of the British in Hong Kong. A second treaty in 1887 granted Portugal possession of the territory for perpetuity, including the offshore islands of Taipa and Coloane.

Macau watched carefully from the sidelines as Dr Sun Yat-sen overthrew the Dragon Throne in 1911 to establish the Republic of China. With Portugal neutral during World War I, Macau found itself on the sidelines of that conflict. This same neutrality prevented a Japanese attack in 1942, and Macau became a tiny island of calm, surrounded by millions of Imperial Japanese troops. It turned into a Casablanca of the Orient, a haven for political refugees, deserters and carpetbaggers; people who were either trying to escape the war or take advantage of the conflict.

The colony should have slipped back into its traditional slumber once the war ended. And it would have, if not for the Bretton Woods Agreement of 1946 which banned the import of gold for private purposes into British possessions. Almost overnight, a thriving gold-smuggling path opened between China, Macau and Hong Kong – a black market that flourished until 1974 when the agreement was repealed.

By 1946, China was engulfed in a bloody revolution. After three years of heavy fighting and the loss of millions of lives, Mao Tse-tung emerged the victor and Kuomintang leader Chiang Kai-shek fled to Taiwan. Thousands of refugees poured into Macau, causing a crisis to the civil authorities. This stream did not stop until 1952 when the Portuguese signed a cooperation agreement with Peking.

Vegas of the East

Macau's modern economic transformation began in 1964 when gambling was legalized and the Sociedade de Turismo e Diversoes de Macau (STDM) was given a monopoly on casinos and other gaming operations. STDM quickly realized that it needed a way for punters to reach Macau and places for them to sleep and eat between forays to the blackjack tables, so it branched into the ferry, hotel and restaurant business.

Casinos and pawn shops jostle for space

Almost overnight, the sleepy city blossomed into a Vegas of the East with flashy neon signs and raunchy floor shows, attracting thousands of Hong Kong gamblers weekly. Gambling revenue funded schools, hospitals and public works projects like the Macaû-Taipa Bridge, which opened in 1974. It also spurred a manufacturing boom, as textile, toy and handicraft factories sprang to life.

The economic boom continued despite persistent trouble with China, which had sunk into the gloom of the Cultural Revolution. Red Guards rampaged through the streets of Macau in 1966 and eight of them died when Portuguese troops fired back. Beijing asked for a public apology and more influence in local politics. At the end of his tender, Governor Carvalho offered to hand the colony back to China. Taken by surprise – and faced with the prospect of losing a valuable source of foreign exchange – Beijing quickly backtracked on its demands.

Macau-Taipa Bridge

In 1974, the Portuguese government was overthrown by a military junta under General Antonio de Spinoza. The new regime quickly went about dismantling the Portuguese empire, granting independence to its colonies; Macau, however, stayed within Lisbon's sphere. Three years later, rumours rocked the colony again: Portugal wanted to divest itself of Macau but China refused to take it back. But nothing concrete transpired until 1987 when the Sino-Portuguese Treaty, an agreement for the return of Macau to Chinese rule in 1999, was signed.

Instead of throwing the colony into a panic, the treaty ignited an economic boom, the likes of which had not been seen since the early 17th century. Business confidence seems to be at an all-time high, with millions of dollars in investment funds pouring in from Hong Kong, Taiwan, Japan, Portugal and even mainland China. The current boom is also fueled by rapid economic growth in Hong Kong and Guangdong Province in southern China.

The powers that be in Macau are laying the foundation for future growth by building a transportation and industrial infrastructure second to none in Asia: a new ferry terminal and a second Macau-Taipa bridge were completed in 1993. A US$1 billion international airport will open on an artificial island east of Taipa in 1995, giving Macau its own window to the world and lessening its dependence on Hong Kong. Along the north coast of Coloane, a huge deep-water container port is taking shape and along the Outer Harbour, the mammoth Praia Project will transform Macau's skyline with a dozen more office towers.

On the verge of the 21st century, Macau appears to be entering a new golden age of peace and prosperity.

Historical Highlights

1498 Portuguese explorer Vasco da Gama pioneers a new route to India around the Cape of Good Hope.

1513 Admiral Jorge Alvares explores the coast of southern China.

1517 Portuguese envoy Tome Pires appears before the Dragon Throne in Peking with a proposal for Sino-Portuguese trade.

1540 Liampo becomes an unofficial base of Portugal's China traders.

1549 Chinese troops destroy Liampo; survivors regroup at Sanchuang, near present-day Macau.

1552 St Francis Xavier dies in Sanchuang after failing to convert the Chinese.

1557 As a reward for banishing pirates from the Pearl River Delta, China cedes Macau to the Portuguese and grants Lisbon monopoly in Canton trade.

1627 The Dutch attack on Macau is repulsed.

1637 China revokes Portuguese monopoly on Canton trade.

1641 Dutch take Malacca; Macau is now the sole Portuguese colony in East Asia.

1717 English and French ships begin using Taipa as a base after they are banned from docking at Canton.

1757 Macau's economy recovers after the Canton merchants' guild grabs exclusive rights to China's foreign trade.

1835 St Paul's Church, its adjacent college and library are destroyed by a fire.

1841 China cedes Hong Kong to the British.

1845 Macau, ruled by the Portuguese viceroy in Goa for more than 300 years, becomes a separate province.

1849 The Governor of Macau is assassinated by Chinese rebels. The Portuguese forces destroy a Chinese border fort and calm is restored.

1862 Portugal and China sign a treaty giving Macau a similar colonial status to Hong Kong.

1887 Second Sino-Portuguese treaty gives Lisbon infinite rights to Macau and the offshore islands of Taipa and Coloane.

1911 Manchu Dynasty collapses and Dr Sun Yat-sen forms the Republic of China.

1928 Mao Tse-tung establishes first guerilla base in China.

1937 Japan invades China to start war in the Pacific.

1941 After attacking Pearl Harbour, Japanese forces pour south into Asia; Macau becomes a neutral enclave.

1949 Communist forces claim victory in China.

1952 Thousands of refugees from Red China flow into Macau; Portugal signs an agreement pledging cooperation with Communist authorities in Beijing.

1954 First grand prix auto race through the streets of Macau.

1964 Legalized gambling starts in Macau.

1966 Cultural Revolution begins in China; Red Guards pour into the streets of Macau.

1967 The Governor of Macau, Carvalho, threatens to quit Portuguese rule in the colony. China backs down on its demands for more political influence there.

1972 Richard Nixon visits China.

1974 Revolution in Portugal; Macau-Taipa Bridge opens.

1981 University of East Asia opens on Taipa Island.

1984 Britain and China sign accord for Hong Kong's return to China in 1997.

1987 Lisbon and Beijing sign a treaty detailing Macau's return to China in 1999.

Day Itin

Three days might seem like a long time to spend in Macau for anyone who isn't a hard-core gambler. However, in spite of its tiny size, the Portuguese colony has an immense variety of attractions and a certain charisma.

The first day is a general introduction to Macau, including many of the primary sights and covering much of the old city and thriving downtown district. The second day takes you to the outer islands, Taipa and Coloane, famous for their beaches, parks and Portuguese restaurants. The third day reveals more of the bygone Macau, a casual stroll along the Inner Harbour through neighbourhoods which have changed little in the last 50 years.

DAY 1

The Praia Grande and Old Macau

Breakfast at the Lisboa Hotel, followed by a stroll along the waterfront past major landmarks.

One of the most recognizable landmarks in Macau is the **Lisboa Hotel and Casino** on the waterfront at the mainland end of the **Macau-Taipa Bridge**. Writers have been trying to describe its unique architecture for several decades, but the overall effect is vintage Las Vegas with a slight Asian touch: a fussy, flamboyant structure that seems to reflect the mood of the gamblers inside.

Noite e Dia Cafe (Tel: 577666) in the hotel offers Western and Chinese dishes round-the-clock. It is one of a few places in town where you can sample a traditional Portuguese breakfast: scrambled eggs made with spicy sausages, garlic bread and espresso. Girls

Lisboa Hotel

from the Crazy Paris show often eat here in the morning. If you don't want a sit-down meal, head for the hotel cake shop with its freshly-baked doughnuts, danish, French bread and sandwiches.

After breakfast, take a look around the Lisboa. Both the casino and hotel lobbies are dominated by immense chandeliers and slightly psychedelic decor. The latter has a collection of rather bizarre reproductions and miniatures: King Tut's gold death mask, gilded baroque tables featuring portraits of Napoleon and Louis XVI, a solid jade junk and a model of the Temple of Heaven done in jade, gold and lapis. The casino is just as quirky: a swarm of frenzied activity as punters test their luck at blackjack, roulette, baccarat and traditional Chinese games like *pai-kao* (dominoes), *dai siu* (big and small) and *fantan* (the button game). And there are hundreds of 'hungry tigers' – the local term for slot machines.

Fronting the casino is a huge roundabout that funnels traffic to and from the bridge. In a way, the square reflects the past and future of Macau. Traffic swirls around an equestrian statue of Portuguese hero Ferreira do Amaral, in the shadow of the towering **Bank of China Building**, a bastion of mainland power that anticipates the 1999 hand-over to China. Completed in 1992, the 38-storey structure is Macau's tallest.

Walk to the right of the bank, along Avenida Infante D Henrique, one of the city's main shopping streets. Sintra Square is on your left; beyond is a block full of late-night pawn shops which are gold and jewellery shops by day. Continue down the road to the intersection **Rua Dr Pedro Jose Lobo**. The block after this intersection features camera shops, electronics outlets and chic boutiques. Dominating the busy intersection ahead is the pink colonial facade of the **National Overseas Bank** (B N Ultramarino), brightly illuminated at night with hundreds of tiny lights.

Turn left onto **Rua da Praia Grande**,

Government House, originally built as a palace

which leads past the **Jorge Alvares Monument** to the waterfront. 'Praia grande' means 'big beach' in Portuguese, a misnomer these days because the strand has disappeared beneath a groan of bulldozers and cranes transforming the bay into one of the largest reclamation projects in Asian history. It is hard to imagine now, but, by the turn of the century, a dozen new office blocks, parks and man-made lagoons will fill the space between Praia Grande and the Macau-Taipa bridge.

The initial section of Praia Grande embraces boutiques and foreign banks, but the most prominent landmark along this part of the waterfront is **Government House**, built in 1849 as the private palace of the Viscount of Cercal but which now houses the offices of the Portuguese governor and his staff. Turn right into a narrow lane called Travessa Padre Narciso and proceed uphill to **St Lawrence's Church** (Sao Lourenco). The faded yellow facade is the most handsome of Macau churches, with twin bell towers flanked by towering palms. The nave has resplendent stained glass, religious statues and a turquoise ceiling framed in yellow and cream.

St Lawrence's Church

Exit down the grand stairway and turn left into Rua de Sao Lourenco. Two blocks down, the street splits into low (Rua Central) and high roads. Take the cobblestoned high road, which winds its way to the richly restored **Dom Pedro V Theatre**. Unveiled in 1859, this was the first European-style theatre in China. It was once the fulcrum of colonial social life in Macau with a busy slate of drama, music and balls. A number of famous operas made their Asian debuts at the Dom Pedro, including *The Barber of Seville*. Nowadays, it is a stage for visiting theatre troupes and the International Music Festival each autumn.

Opposite is **St Augustine's Church** (Santo Agostinho), a simple building with a pleasant yellow facade. Behind the altar is a famous statue of Christ bearing the cross. This is taken down and carried through the streets of Macau on the first Sunday of Lent during the procession of Our Lord of the Passion (Nosso Senhor dos Passos), Macau's most important Catholic celebration. The present church was built in 1814, replacing a 16th-century chapel. West of the church is a leafy plaza called **Largo de Santo Agostinho**, surrounded by old colonial buildings like St Joseph's Seminary, Casa Ricci (a Jesuit charity) and the Sir Robert Ho Tung Library of the Cultural Institute of Macau.

The road ahead, Calcada Tronco Velho, leads downhill to Macau's most important square, the **Largo do Senado**, which is crowded with people at all times of the day. The **General Post Office** is the large gray building on the eastern side, next to a delicate white-washed facade of the **Holy House of Mercy** (Santa Casa da Misericordia), a Catholic charity that has been in Macau since 1568. The western edge is bounded by a restored colonial building with a long arcade, which houses the visitor centre of the **Macau Government Tourist Office** (MGTO). The small street to the left of MGTO leads into **St Dominic's Market**. You can buy fresh vegetables, fruit, meat, fish, flowers and clothes here.

Dominating the southern flank of the square is the **Leal Senado** (Loyal Senate), perhaps the finest example of Iberian architecture in Macau. The Senate was established in 1583 as a body of local businessmen and dignitaries who advised the Portuguese governor. Until the early 19th century, the board functioned as the de facto colonial government. But it was downgraded in 1833 to a city council. Today, the Senate oversees various urban functions from garbage collection to parks and recreation. The Leal Senado, which was built in 1784, houses a number of interesting sections including an art gallery, a small concert hall, a lovely central courtyard with a garden and a teak-panelled library with a collection of rare books relating to Macau and China. Admission is free to its lobby (Monday–Friday 9am–1pm and 3pm–5.30pm; Saturday 9am–12.30pm), garden, gallery (during exhibitions only) and library (Monday–Saturday 1–8pm).

The Iberian-inspired Leal Senado (Loyal Senate)

Time for lunch. Facing right onto the square (next to the black-and-white cow sign) is **Long Kei** (Tel: 573970), one of the oldest and most venerable Cantonese restaurants in Macau. The menu is extensive, with nearly 400 items including fresh seafood and vegetables. After lunch, stroll down Macau's 'main street', **Avenida Almeida Ribeiro** or **San Ma Lo** as the Chinese call it. The street runs between the Inner Harbour and Praia Grande, cutting a busy swathe across the peninsula. It is lined with pawnshops, jewellery stores, clothing outlets and restaurants. At the corner of **Travessa do Matadouro** is a stall selling old coins, stamps and banknotes. Two blocks from its western terminus is **Kam Pek Casino**, an old Chinese gambling hall frequented mostly by locals. Also stroll down **Rua Camilo Pessanha,** where there is a traditional Chinese medicine shop and a wonderful old Portuguese building called the **Casa de Beneficiencia Tung Sin Tong**.

Retrace your steps to Largo do Senado and head north past the row of restored colonial buildings. The square grows tighter on both sides, but after another block it re-emerges in a small plaza fronting the **Church of St Dominic** (Sao Domingo). The facade looks a bit rundown, but don't let that fool you: this is the most exquisite church in Macau. The baroque altar is resplendent with gold ornaments, ornate plasterwork and effigies of various saints, with a statue of the Virgin and Child at the centre. St Dominic's was first built in the 1590s, but the present structure dates from the early 17th century. The church is always locked. To enter, press the bell on the gate to the right of the facade.

St Dominic's Church

Once you have viewed the interior, cross the square in front of the church past the parked pedicabs and walk up a dark and narrow lane called the Travessa do Sao Domingo to yet another small European-style square: **Largo da Se**. Towering above the parked cars and trees is **Macau Cathedral** (the Se), the mother church of the Macau diocese but rather staid when compared with some of the smaller chapels. The present church dates from 1937, the latest in a sequence of cathedrals on this site since the late 16th century.

Exit the square via a tiny street called Travessa da Se, walking a block to **Rua Sao Domingos**, one of the city's most fashionable shopping streets. Straight ahead is busy Rua Palha, flanked by clothing and shoe shops and always crowded with pedestrian and auto traffic. Follow Rua Palha for about 250m (820ft), until you see the wreckage of St Paul's.

Although it lies in ruins, **St Paul's Church** (Sao Paulo) is Macau's most enduring symbol and most popular landmark. It was once the grandest church in the Orient, completed in the early 17th century with a stone facade carved by Japanese Christians under the direction of Italian architect-priest Carlo Spinola. Next door was the Jesuit College, the first West-

Rua Sao Domingos

ern-style university in Asia and a place where missionaries learnt to speak Chinese before venturing into China.

Gawking at St Paul's

All but the facade was destroyed by fire in 1835 and never rebuilt. Nevertheless, the facade is a masterpiece of baroque art and a tribute to the Portuguese presence in Asia: stone dragons and sailing ships, angels and devils and even a depiction of the Garden of Eden adorn it. People swarm the steps of St Paul's all day, and the square below is packed with souvenir stalls and antique shops.

Rising even higher than St Paul's is a stout bastion called **Monte Fort** (daily 7am–sunset, free admission), or the Fortress of Sao Paulo do Monte. A footpath leads through a small park and around the southern bastion to the entrance gate of the fort, where there is a MGTO information office and a small shrine to the Virgin and Child.

The citadel dates from the early 17th century, a virtual 'city within a city'. With large cisterns and food stores, it was built to withstand a siege of up to two years. The primary construction material was *chunambo* – a blend of earth, straw, lime and oyster shells – that was nearly impervious to cannon balls. The foundation is solid granite.

Monte's powerful cannons could hit targets in the Outer Harbour and across the Chinese border. But they were only fired once, during a Dutch attack in 1627. A force of Jesuits and black African slaves drove the invaders back into the sea with a lucky cannon shot that destroyed the Dutch powder magazine. The 1835 fire that destroyed the church also scorched most of the buildings inside the fort. The only unscathed structure is now a meteorological station.

The best cannons are along the southern wall, which also con-

Sunset vistas from Monte Fort

tains various Portuguese crests and inscriptions, plus a reproduction of the original Monte bell that called men to arms. There are stunning views from every bastion: over St Paul's, Camoes Garden, the Inner Harbour, Lappa Island in China, the downtown skyline and across to Guia Lighthouse.

You can linger until the fort closes at sunset, or retrace your steps past the ruins of St Paul's back into the heart of the old town. To round off a well-spent day, take a 10-minute walk to **Restaurant Portugues** at 16 Rua do Campo for dinner.

Taipa and Coloane Islands

Drive or take the bus to Macau's outer islands, visit Hac Sa (Black Sand) Beach and see a bone relic of St Francis Xavier.

You can walk around the outer islands, but it would take several days. Wheeled transport, on the other hand, allows you to discover both Taipa and Coloane between breakfast and dinner. Mokes are the best way to see the islands: you can explore at your own speed. You can also take the bus or taxi. Public buses No 11, 21 and 21A run between the mainland and the outer islands; bus No 14 connects Coloane and Taipa villages.

Another option is cycling and you can rent bikes from half a dozen stalls in Taipa Village. See *Practical Information.*

Aerial view of Taipa Island

Once you have decided on your form of transport, it is time to start the tour. If you have not eaten yet, **A Pousada** (Tel: 831234) at the Hyatt Regency Hotel is one of the more pleasant places in Taipa to have breakfast. The cafe has a conservatory setting with glass ceilings and walls that look out on the garden and across the bay. The cafe serves Continental, American and Chinese food. If feeling especially lucky, duck into the hotel's **Taipa Casino** – even at the crack of dawn there are eager punters hunched over the tables in rapt concentration.

Taipa and Coloane Islands

2 km / 1.25 miles

After breakfast, continue east along Estrada Almirante Marques Esparteiro, a four-lane highway that slices across Taipa Island. The first sight on your left is the New Century Hotel with its huge neon sign. On the ridge behind is the **University of Macau** (formerly University of East Asia). The university theatre is a venue for the International Music Festival each fall. It also hosts distinguished guest speakers from time to time, among which were former US Secretary of State Henry Kissinger and famous American broadcaster Walter Cronkite.

Tou Tei, the Earth God

The middle of Taipa was filled with rice paddies and duck farms until the early 1990s when the Macau government and private developers began transforming the rural landscape with modern high-rise housing to alleviate crowded conditions on the peninsula. Massive condo developments now fill the gap between the Hyatt and Taipa village.

Turn left at the junction of Estrada Almirante and Estrada Nova and follow the two-lane highway around the northern edge of Taipa to the **United Chinese Cemetery**. Public buses No 11, 22, 28A and 33 run from the Hyatt Regency to the cemetery. The closest bus stop is about five minutes' walk from the entrance. Thousands of graves sprawl across the hillside, facing the open sea (the most auspicious position according to Chinese tradition). A huge mosaic statue of **Tou Tei**, the Earth God, overlooks the scene, gazing out at the new **Taipa-Macau Bridge** and the site of the new international airport.

The four-lane bridge, completed in late 1993, takes the pressure of bumper-to-bumper traffic off the old bridge during peak hours. It will eventually connect the airport terminals to mainland Macau and China. **Macau International Airport**, scheduled to open in 1995, is likely to be one or two years late. When completed, it will feature a passenger terminal with separate customs and immigration for Macau and Hong Kong, a cargo terminal and a large aircraft maintenance facility. The runway is being constructed on an artificial island between Taipa and Coloane, one of the largest civil engineering projects in Asia. Total cost: nearly US$1 billion.

Follow the road around the island's eastern shore to the Taipa-Coloane Causeway, or retrace your steps to the bus stop and board bus No 21A. Located across the shallow strait is

The old Macau-Taipa Bridge

The beautiful Hac Sa Beach

Coloane Island, nearly twice the size of Taipa but with a fraction of the population. Coloane functions as Macau's nature and outdoor recreation hub. If you have your own transport, turn left after the causeway and follow the road over the wooded ridge and around for 3km (1¾ miles) to **Hac Sa Beach**. Otherwise, stay on the bus until it reaches its terminus in the beach parking lot.

Hac Sa (Black Sand) Beach is one of the most beautiful stretches of the south China coast, a curving strand with soft dark sand set in a framework of pines and lush green hills. The water is often muddy with silt from the Pearl River, but it is free of the industrial pollution that plagues Hong Kong's beaches. Windsurfers and small sailboats can be hired at two kiosks along the beach, and horses can be rented at the **Macau Riding Centre**. The adjacent **Hac Sa Sports and Recreation Complex** has an olympic-sized pool, miniature golf course and roller-skating rink.

About ¾km (½ mile) from the complex, commanding a small cape at the north end of the beach is the **Westin Resort** (Tel: 871111), the island's largest hotel and Macau's newest deluxe property. The ochre-coloured rooms rise in terraces amid lush tropical gardens, bringing a touch of the Mexican Riviera to the China coast. Directly behind the hotel is the new **Macau Golf and Country Club**, with an 18-hole championship course and grass tennis courts. The club is open only to members and Westin Resort guests.

The road around the southern edge of Coloane leads to **Cheoc Van Beach**, which looks more like the Mediterranean than any other part of Macau. About 1½km (¾ mile) from Hac Sa Beach, it has luxury condos. The **Pousada de Coloane** hotel scales the hillside behind the boat club, which has kayaks, sailboats and windsurfers for hire. Cheoc Van faces the open ocean, so the surf is much rougher than at Hac Sa. But you can swim at the adjacent public pool (daily 9 am–10 pm). Cheoc Van is a regular stop on the bus No 21A route between Hac Sa Beach and Coloane Village.

Coloane Village lies around the headland, on the edge of a placid bay that faces Lappa Island in China. Take bus No 21A there. The village is best explored on foot. Until 1910, this village was still attacked by Chinese pirates and even today, there is a sleepy, bygone feel about it. The locals make a living off the tourist trade, as well as by fishing and boat-building.

At the waterfront's southern end is **Tam Kong Temple**, a typical maritime shrine dedi-

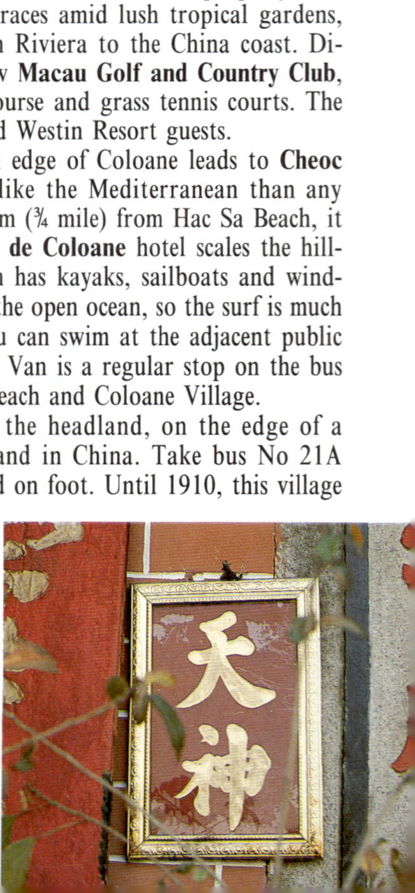

Tam Kong Temple

cated to the Goddess of the Sea. Buddhist gods occupy centrestage, with great coils of incense suspended from the wooden-beam ceiling. The most unusual item inside the temple is a 1-m long whale bone carved in the shape of a dragon boat, complete with oarsmen.

But the village's most famous sight is the **Church of St Francis Xavier**, a modest cream-coloured building facing a leafy plaza. With its typical baroque facade, the church looks several centuries old, but it was actually built in 1928. Inside are numerous sacred relics, including a bone from the arm of St Francis Xavier who died near Macau in 1552. The tiny fragment is kept in a silver reliquary in a side chapel and you must ask the resident priest for permission to see it. The church also contains the holy remains of a few Catholic martyrs who were killed in Japan and Indochina.

A bone relic of St Francis Xavier is kept here

In the plaza outside is a small cement **obelisk** which commemorates a 1910 battle between local authorities and marauding pirates – the last pirate attack on Macau. The victory is celebrated with a festival in the village on 13 July each year. Just around the corner is the **Coloane public library** with its harvest gold facade, another superb example of colonial architecture.

Further north along the waterfront are Coloane's famous **junk yards**, about a dozen active boat-building sheds where fishing trawlers and *sampans* take shape. Most of the boats are bound for fishing fleets in Hong Kong. The yards are suffused with the smell of freshly-cut wood and the persistent din of ancient carpentry tools. Nobody minds if you wander through the yards and the workmen are quite proud if you snap pictures of their craft.

Coloane village is a good place to stop for lunch. There are several outdoor cafes along the square in front of St Francis Xavier Church and several more at the traffic roundabout in the middle of town. **Cacarola Restaurant** (Tel: 328226) at the main square is a local Portuguese favourite with dishes like African chicken and cod. Food is very cheap and good here.

Three different bus lines (Nos 14, 21, 21A) run along the east coast of Coloane. About five minutes from the village centre is a turn-off on the right to **Alto Coloane**, at 174m (570ft) the highest point in the Portuguese territory. There are no buses to the top – walk or take a taxi. The road winds through typical coastal terrain, with thick bush and coniferous trees set against orange soil. The viewpoint at the summit offers stunning views of the surrounding islands and water, and there are several nearby picnic spots maintained by the Forestry Department.

A popular hiking route called the **Coloane Trail** loops 8½km (5 miles) around the mountain; the trail can be reached from the summit or its official starting point near the bottom of the hill, just above the police barracks. The trail terminus also has a formal exercise and jogging course.

Follow the mountain road back to the spot where it intersects the coastal road and make a right turn. Just ahead is the entrance to **Coloane Park**, which also has a botanical garden, a playground and an aviary with more than 200 species of Southeast Asian and Chinese birds.

Cross the causeway again (bus No 14) and follow Estrada Almirante, which forks to the left. Taipa Village is just ahead. But the village roads are all one-way, which means that both cars and buses must go all the way to the Almirante-Nova junction before doubling back along a narrow lane called Rua Carlos Eugenio into the heart of the village.

The main bus and taxi stop is **Largo Governador Barbosa**, a big square surrounded by bicycle shops. It is best to walk from here, as many of the village streets are closed to vehicular traffic. Wander at will through the back lanes, where life seems to have changed little in the past century. **Rua de Mercadores** is one of the more fascinating streets, with pastel-coloured houses and shops that would not look out of place along the Algarve Coast. But just to remind you that this is still Asia, the **Pak Tai Temple** sits at the very centre of the village with its coils of burning incense and golden gods. Another temple is close to the waterfront, dedicated to Tin Hau, the Protector of Fishermen.

Rua do Cunha is Taipa's most famous lane – often called **Food Street** because of its myriad eating places. By day, the street is given over to elderly street merchants who sell fresh fruits, vegetables and sugar cane. There is also an old Chinese medicine shop and several other traditional stores. But after dark, Rua do Cunha becomes a blaze of neon lights as the restaurants come to life.

The old Portuguese quarter is a short walk to the east, via either of two routes: Rua Carlos Eugenio and Calcado do

Fresh produce for the picking

Carmo, or Avenida de Carlos Maia, which does a sharp hairpin turn in front of the police academy on Canhao Revolver Hill. Either way, you end up in the cobblestoned plaza in front of **Our Lady of Carmel Church** (Nossa Senhora do Carmo), one of the least-known but most beautiful chapels in Macau. Christened in 1885, the church crowns a hill with a fine view of the sea and the waterfront with its stately mansions. Beyond the row of colonial buildings on the opposite side of the square is **Carmel Garden**, a small European-style garden.

Avenida da Praia runs directly along the shore, beneath towering banyan trees and a row of exquisite mansions in which Macanese aristocrats once lived. The homes date from the early 20th century and they are primarily Portuguese-style, with wide verandas, louvred wooden window shutters, high ceilings and plaster facades painted light green with white trim. Much of the original furniture is of Chinese origin: dark rosewood and carved with typical Asian figures like dragons and lions. Only one mansion is open to the public – the **Taipa House Museum** (Tel: 327088; Tuesday–Sunday 9.30am–1pm, 3–5.30pm) which is the second from the end. The last house is the residence of the mayor of Taipa.

The tour is over, but you can linger in Taipa Village until dinner, selecting from one of the dozen restaurants along Rua do Cunha and nearby lanes. Taxis are easy to catch from either of the main village squares, or you can hop on the No 11 bus back to mainland Macau.

DAY 3

The Inner Harbour: Camoes Garden to Barra Point

Explore the bustling waterfront of the Inner Harbour and lunch at a Portuguese restaurant.

There is no place to breakfast around Camoes Garden, so eat at your hotel before starting out. Start your tour at a leafy plaza, **Camoes Square**, which can be reached easily by taxi from anywhere in Macau. Alternatively, take public bus No 3A from the Ferry Terminal or outside the Lisboa Hotel; change to the minibus No 18 at Rua Mercadores or outside the Floating Casino.

Camoes Square is the focus of a number of interesting sights, but start with the **Old Protestant Cemetery** on the eastern flank of the square. This is one of the most tranquil spots in Macau with lovely palms, pines and frangipani trees, and ivy crawling up the walls.

Founded in the 1820s, the graveyard contains the remains of people who died in Macau or surrounding Chinese territory in the late 18th and early 19th centuries. Most were mariners engaged in China trade or military operations, but you will also find the graves of missionaries, housewives and children who died far away from home. They represent many nationalities including British, German, Dutch, Danish and Australian. A surprising number were American sailors from good seafaring towns like Sag Harbour, New Haven, Salem and Boston.

Two of the more noteworthy graves belong to George Chinnery and Lord Henry John Spencer Churchill. Born in London in 1774, Chinnery spent much of his life in Asia where he immortalized a romantic vision of the Orient with his paintings of sweeping vistas of clipper ships, junks and fishing villages. He died in 1852 at No 8 Rua de Inacio Baptista, Macau, and there is now a large monument to his memory at the rear of the cemetery. Lord Henry, great-uncle of Winston Churchill, was the captain of a British ship, the *Druid*, when he died of a tropical disease in 1840.

The small building near the cemetery entrance is **Morrison Chapel**, a modest but inspiring church named after missionary Robert Morrison who translated the Bible into Chinese. There are old photos and memorial stones inside, plus a map and index to the surrounding cemetery. Holy communion services in English are held at 9am on the first and third Sundays of each month.

Turn right from the cemetery gate and pass beneath an old archway into the grounds of **Casa Garden** (daily 9.30am–6pm), a handsome Portuguese villa that was formerly called the Camoes Museum. Admission is free, but you must sign in and collect a badge at the guard house. The exhibits on the upper floor change about once a year, but normally include ancient Chinese ceramics and drawings or paintings by Chinnery. The museum is managed by the Lisbon-based Orient Foundation (Fundacao Oriente) which strives to strengthen cultural and linguistic links between Portugal and various Asian communities that have historical links with Portugal.

Although it is now a public museum, Casa Garden is the oldest surviving private residence in Macau. Built in the 18th century, the house was leased by local chairmen of the British East India Company from 1785 to 1833 when the company charter was revoked by the Portuguese administration. It was later used as an ammunition magazine and as government printers before being converted into a museum in 1960.

Directly west of the museum is the famous **Camoes Garden**, the city's best-known green space. It was once part of the grounds of the adjacent Casa Garden, but after the British were evicted in the

Six is a crowd, Camoes Gardens

1830s it reverted to local Portuguese lodgers. In 1886, the area became the colony's first public park, a rambling woody confine that hugs the contours of a rocky knoll.

Chinese families crowd Camoes Garden on weekends, when it is sometimes difficult to find an empty bench. Weekdays are more placid, as the park is taken over by elderly residents from the surrounding neighbourhood who come for a casual chat, a game of Chinese checkers or a stroll around the grounds with their prized songbirds housed in delicate bamboo cages. If you get here early enough, you can see people practising an ancient form of shadow boxing called *taiji*. Throughout the day, Chinese fortune tellers offer their services at wooden tables just outside the garden entrance.

At the highest point in the garden are the remains of an 18th-century observatory built by French astronomer and cartographer La Perouse. And at the very back of the park is a statue of St Andre Kim (1821–46), the first Korean priest, who studied at the Roman Catholic Procurate in Macau before he was martyred in his homeland. But the garden's most important landmark is the **Camoes Grotto**, carved from bare stone and jungle as a monument to Luis de Camoes. Portugal's most famous poet, he is thought to have lived in Macau in 1557. There is a bronze bust of Camoes and huge granite slabs bearing an inscription of his *Sonnet to Macau*.

On the south side of Camoes Square is the rather sombre-looking **Church of St Anthony** (Santo Antonio) There has been a place of worship on this site since 1558, when the original St Anthony's was erected as the first Roman Catholic church in Macau. The building has been destroyed several times by fire, and the current structure dates from the 1930s. A captain in the Portuguese army who later became a soldier of God, St Anthony is one of the official 'protectors' of Macau. Every year, on June 13, the President of the Macau Senate presents a statue of the saint with religious offerings for protecting the territory during the preceding year.

After visiting St Anthony's, walk directly out of the front gates of the churchyard and down the hill via an old street called **Calcada Botelho**. There are a number of interesting shops along the way. At No 2D is Long Fei, a Chinese pottery and porcelain store, and just beyond is an incense shop called Ian Wo Papelaria. Antiquario Veng Koi at No 6A has a selection of ceramics and other antiques, and at the bottom of the block is an old rice shop with the grain displayed in big wooden bins. There is a traditional Chi-

Inner harbour scene

nese pharmacy at No 27B. Calcada Botelho becomes Rua do Tarrafeiro at this point and runs down to the inner harbour. A street artist often sets up shop at the corner of Tarrafeiro and Rua de Cinco Outubro, and just before you reach the waterfront road there is a rickety wooden stall on the right which shelters street barbers.

Rua do Tarrafeiro ends at a broad waterfront road called Rua Visconde Paco de Arcos, which runs along the edge of the **Inner Harbour** (Porto Interior). Cross the road carefully and turn left, walking south along the docks, past several large cargo piers (pontes). Just beyond Pier 21 is a landing place for *sampans* that take passengers across the harbour to the city of Wanzai on Lappa Island in mainland China. Until a few years ago, Wanzai was a tranquil fishing village, but the economic boom in southern China has ushered in an era of frantic building, resulting in new high-rise hotels, offices and apartments on the western shore of the Inner Harbour. Foreign passport holders are not allowed to cross into China at this point, so give up any hope of crossing by *sampan*. A floating restaurant is anchored offshore at this point.

Further south is a busy intersection where several major streets come together. **Avenida Almeida Ribeiro** runs southeast through the heart of downtown Macau, while Rua das Lorchas heads south along the rest of the waterfront. Overlooking the junction are the **Grand Hotel** and Pier 16's art deco **clock tower**, which no longer works. If you are hungry, the **Grand Hotel** has a small cafe (8am–8pm) which serves both Western and Chinese dishes.

The outer edge of Rua das Lorchas embraces piers, warehouses, factories and the **Macau Palace**, a floating casino housed in the body of a converted ferry. This is one of the more unusual places to test your luck at blackjack and baccarat. You can also try Chinese gambling games like *dai siu* and *fantan*. The casino is open 24 hours. The inner (eastern) side of Rua das Lorchas has an eclectic collection of nitty gritty shops including dried seafood outlets, pawnshops, ship chandlers, auto workshops and hardware stores. There are lots of street stalls

Fishermen's model home, Maritime Museum

too, selling fresh fruit, seafood, joss sticks and Chinese pancakes. Wedged between No 131 and 132 is a small neighbourhood temple with coiled incense and fierce-looking effigies.

Further down, the waterfront street changes names to Rua do Almirante Sergio. This is a good time to break for lunch. **A Lorcha** at No 289 (Tel: 313193, lunch 1–3pm, closed at lunchtime on Tuesdays) may be one of Macau's newer Portuguese restaurants, but already it has a good reputation for its dishes like caldo verde soup, African chicken, cod and spicy prawns.

A-Ma Temple

Walk south to a wide square flanked by a restored colonial building, an ancient temple and the new **Maritime Museum** (daily 10am–5pm, except Tuesday), one of the best in Asia. The museum is a treasure trove of seafaring models and displays. Its top floor houses a small aquarium with marine animals from local waters. You can learn all sorts of interesting facts about Macau: that the 1874 typhoon was the worst recorded, causing more than 1,000 deaths and 100 shipwrecks; that US bombers destroyed the Macau seaplane base in 1945 to prevent the Japanese from using it.

The museum has a small flotilla of ships including an authentic dragon boat, an old tug and replica of a Portuguese *lorcha*, ships which dominated Far East trade in the 16th century. The *lorcha* is used for harbour cruises on Saturday, Sunday and Monday. The journey takes about 30 minutes, a fascinating round trip through the Inner Harbour that affords a close-up view of fishing boats and cargo ships. Cruise times are: 10.30am, 11.30am, 3.30pm, 4.30pm. Further north, in the wide bay between the mainland and Green Island (Ilha Verde), the boat cruises past junk-building yards and a water village on stilts called **Bairro Fai Chi Kei**.

Across the square is **A-Ma Temple**, the city's oldest house of worship and the place that gave Macau its name. Dedicated to A-Ma, the Taoist Goddess of the Sea, there has been a temple on this site since the 15th century, when fisherman from the Fujian province in eastern

China settled on the peninsula. They called the place A-Ma Gau (A-Ma Bay) which the Portuguese corrupted to Macau when they arrived a century later. The temple precinct climbs a good deal of the way up Penha Hill, with four distinct units and various small shrines in between. Firecrackers are often set off in the main courtyard, which also contains a boulder with a painting of the junk that allegedly brought the Goddess A-Ma to the Pearl River region. The main shrine has a huge round window that looks out over the harbour and Lappa Island on the far side, but there are even better views further up the hillside.

The last part of the route follows the contours of **Barra Point**. You can walk – it takes about 15 minutes to reach the tip of the peninsula – or catch a pedicab from in front of the temple or museum. Either way, you pass the mustard-coloured walls of the **Naval Dockyard**, where the marine police moor their speedboats. **Barra Fort** was once the most important stronghold in Macau, protecting the entrance to the Inner Harbour. Finished in 1629, the fort had 24 cannons (50- and 24-pounders) and a 60-strong garrison. In 1740, a small chapel was added to the fort, in dedication to St James (Sao Tiago), the patron saint of warriors and other military men. But over the past hundred years, as the threat to Portuguese rule declined, much of the citadel was demolished.

Barra Fort was taken over by the Macau Government Tourist Office (MGTO) in 1976 and transformed into an exquisitely romantic hotel called the **Pousada de Sao Tiago** (Tel: 378111). The 23-room hotel is believed to be haunted by a statue of St James which, in the old days, purportedly got off its pedestal every night to inspect the fort. Each morning, a soldier would be assigned to clean the mud off and polish the statue's boots. Many of the original features of the fort have been incorporated into the present hotel. Linger until sunset, sipping wine or port at its outdoor cafe. The posh **Fortaleza Restaurant** offers gourmet Portuguese food, or you can return to town for dinner.

To return to central Macau, take the bus, taxi, or pedicab along the Praia Grande.

The fort-turned-hotel Pousada de Sao Tiago

Pick & Mix

Morning Itineraries

1. Government Quarter Tour

A historic jaunt through Macau's military and Government Quarter, the Suzhou-style Lou Lim Iok Garden, followed by Dr Sun Yat-Sen Memorial House.

Start early in the morning from beneath the huge neon sign that marks the entrance to **Lisboa Casino**, walking north along Avenida do Dr Rodrigo Rodrigues and beneath the overpass Rua do Campo. You will pass the elaborate pink-and-white facade of the **Military Club**, built in 1870 as the officers' club for the nearby barracks.

Just beyond the club is the lower entrance to **St Francis Garden** (Sao Francisco), a lush green space that crawls up and over the crest of a small bluff. Stairs and walkways climb past open-air pavilions and terraces. The haunt of lovers at night, the garden is a boisterous playground each morning, filled with children from the nearby St Rosa de Lima College. Its upper gardens are dominated by a round tower which resembles a powder magazine, but which is actually a memorial to Macanese soldiers who died in World War I.

St Francis Garden

From the round tower, look right and you will see the **St Francis Barracks**, opposite the Military Club. The barracks were once the fulcrum of army life in Macau but are now the headquarters of the police and security forces. The Portuguese built a solid fort on this site in 1629 to protect the eastern flank of the Praia Grande. Within its walls was a Franciscan monastery and among the powerful armaments was a culverin cannon that could shoot a 16-kg (35-lb) iron ball more than 2km (1¼ miles). Both the

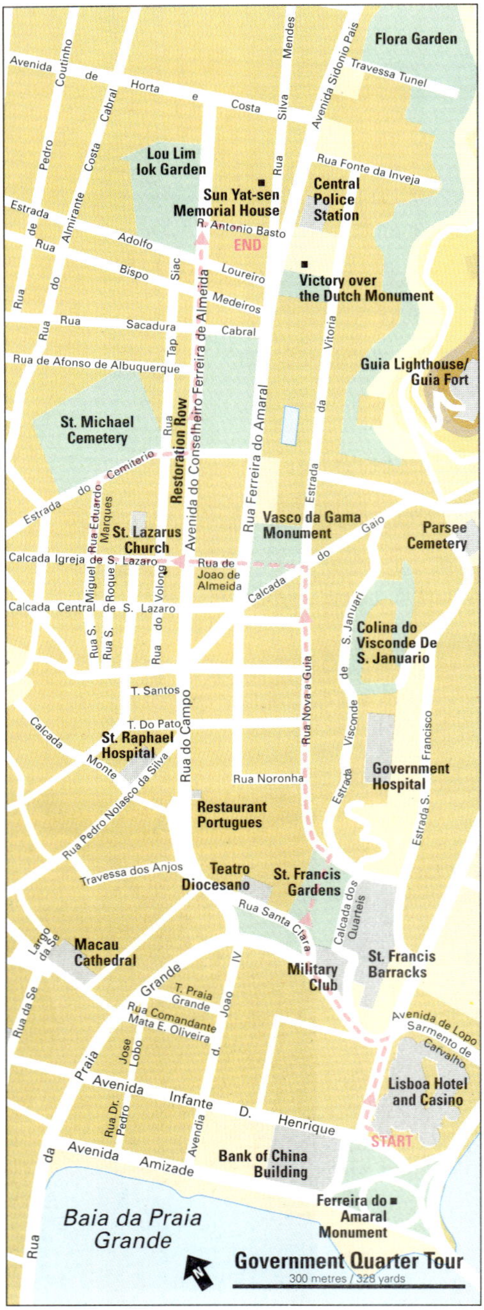

fort and monastery were demolished in 1864 to make way for the barracks one sees today.

Turn left from the gardens and walk along a quiet residential street called **Rua Nova A Guia**. At No 46A is **Vu Fung Antiquario**, a shop selling antique and reproduction Chinese rosewood furniture and camphor chests. Further along, at No 28, is a small shop selling old stamps, coins and paper money. The narrow street suddenly emerges into daylight at **Vasco da Gama Square**, with four old Portuguese cannons and a monument to the 15th-century mariner who first sailed between Europe and Asia via the southern tip of Africa.

Several narrow streets run west from Vasco da Gama Square, but take Rua de Joao de Almeida, which leads into the heart of the **St Lazarus District**, filled with many old buildings that have never been restored. **St Lazarus Church** (Sao Lazaro) is a stout cinderblock chapel with a green trim. The building dates from 1885, but there has been a church here since 1570 when the original St Lazarus was built to serve a leper colony called the Hermitage of Our Lady of Hope. All that remains of the 16th-century shrine is the Cross of Hope in the courtyard. Old women sell flowers from the sidewalk in front of St Lazarus and an ice-cream vendor is present during school days. Behind the church is a large Roman Catholic school called **San Jose College**. Across the street is the **Macau Interparochial Centre**, a flamboyant Iberian-style building with plaster arches, wrought-iron balconies, wooden window shutters and a bell-tower topped with a weather vane.

The next street beyond the church is Rua Eduardo Marques, which leads one block north to the entrance of **St Michael's Cemetery**, a Roman Catholic burial ground with a fine mock-Gothic chapel. Some of the tombs are built in the shape of the traditional 'womb tombs' found in Buddhist cemeteries.

Follow the Estrada do Cemiterio east along the edge of the old graveyard and turn left into Avenida do Conselheiro Ferreira de Almeida, a busy street that cuts a swath across the middle of Macau. On the eastern side of the street is a huge playground with artificial grass, while the western side is dominated by fastidiously renovated colonial mansions – the city's **Restoration Row**. Various government and quasi-public bodies occupy the refurbished spaces including the **Central Library**, **National Archives**, **Portuguese Language Society** and **Oriental Institute**. Most of the buildings date from the early 1920s: two-storey mansions with arches, balustrades, columns and carved capitols, their facades painted in shades of yellow, white and dark red. The houses were slated for demolition in the 1970s when the Macau government proposed to renovate the entire row under a building conservation concept called 'adaptive re-use' in which old structures are put to modern use.

Restoration Row ends at the intersection of Avenida do Conselheiro Ferreira de Almeida and Estrada de Adolfo Loureiro. Turn left and walk about 100m (109yds) to the entrance of **Lou Lim Iok Garden**, which took shape in the late 19th century at the behest of Lou Kan, a wealthy Chinese merchant. After his death in 1906, the garden and adjacent house passed to his eldest son, Lou Lim Iok. By the late 1930s the family was broke; the house was sold and converted into a school but the garden was neglected, taken over by weeds. The Macau government came to its rescue in 1974.

Entering Lou Lim Iok Garden is like walking through a time

Restoration Row

warp into mainland China as it was 50 years ago or more. Fashioned after the famous gardens of Suzhou (Soochow) in China, the park offers a study of nature in miniature: paths meander around the edge of a lotus pond, through bamboo groves illuminated with murky green light, beneath towering banyan trees and grottos sculpted from rough concrete. A sinuous bridge snakes its way across the pond in nine curves – a way to trick demons who can travel only in straight lines. There are always people around: geriatric Macanese practising *taiji* or members of the local Chinese opera troupe rehearsing.

Return to Estrada de Adolfo Loureiro and walk around the corner to Rua Ferreira do Amaral. **Dr Sun Yat-sen Memorial House** (daily 10am–1pm, 2.30–5pm, closed Tuesday) is a tribute to the nationalist leader who led the revolution that overthrew the Manchu (Qing) Dynasty in 1911. Although he never lived in this house, Sun worked as a young intern at Kiang Vu Hospital in Macau for two years (1892–93). During this time, he began agitating for political reform in China. The house contains photos, papers, clothing and furniture once used by Sun, including his marching orders to General Chiang Kai-shek and his transcripts from medical school in Hong Kong. Free admission.

From here, you can plug into the Three Colinas tour (see *Afternoon Itinerary 3*) after lunch via the nearby **Flora Garden** or return downtown on the No 9 bus via Rua Ferreira do Amaral.

2. Old Tercena District

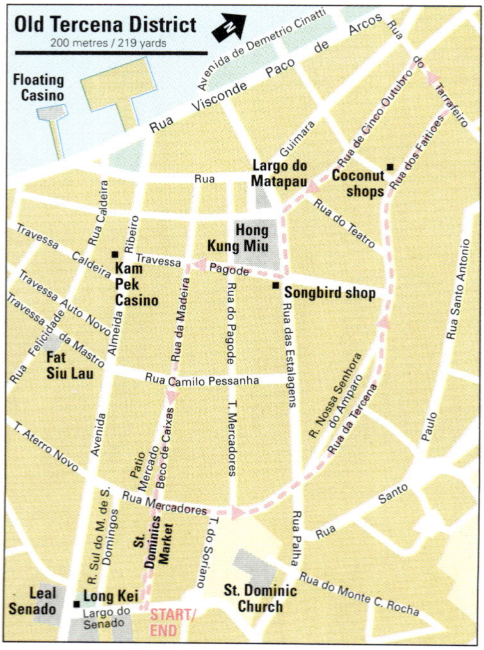

A casual exploration of Tercena District between St Paul's and the Inner Harbour, a warren of narrow streets and alleys filled with antique stores, workshops and street markets.

Tercena is one of the most fascinating parts of old Macau, yet it is still relatively unknown to tourists. Starting from **Largo de Senado square**, cut through **St Dominic's Market** and turn right onto Rua Mercadores with its rice merchants, boutiques, Chinese medicine and herb stores, gold and jade dealers, and fresh produce stalls. After about 150m (164yds), the street curves gently to the west and becomes **Rua da Tercena**. Starting with a shop called Art Culto Religioso Yu Yi at the corner of Tercena and Estalagens, there are antique and furniture dealers on either side of the road. You can buy camphor chests, smaller wooden boxes, rosewood living room sets and dining tables, various bits and bobs of porcelain, and brass buddhas here.

Running parallel to Rua da Tercena is a narrow pedestrian lane called **Rua Nossa Senhora do Amparo**, one of the most fascinating streets in old Macau. There are all sorts of things for sale here: tropical aquarium fish, joss-sticks, jade pendants, gold jewellery, camphor chests and ceramics.

Chinese bric-abrac

An impromptu **flea market** (2pm–7pm) is set up at the western end of Tercena and Amparo each day. Most of the merchants are elderly men who spread their wares on the ground atop blankets, towels and jackets. You will find the usual selection of old coins, jade and porcelain but there are also more unusual items like musical instruments, paper money, wooden abacus sets and old-fashioned typewriters.

Cheap designer sportswear

Rua da Tercena turns into **Rua dos Faitioes**, famous for its fresh coconut shops. At the end of the street turn left into Rua do Tarrafeiro, walk one block and turn left into Rua Cinco de Outubro, a sprawling **street market** spanning nine blocks. There are loads of fresh fruit stalls, but the real attraction here is factory outlets selling designer sportswear, jeans and children's clothes made in Macau. Prices are lower than similar street markets in Hong Kong. Bargain hard anyway.

Dried meat, Rua Cinco de Outubro

About 200m (218yds) down Rua Cinco de Outubro is **Largo do Matapau**, a large open square filled with market stalls. Facing the square is an ancient neighbourhood temple called **Hong Kung Miu** (Temple of the Bazaar). This is a typical Taoist shrine, with prayer halls set around a central courtyard and various golden gods on altars beneath dark wooden-beamed roofs.

Old world charm at Beco de Caixas

After leaving the temple, turn right and follow **Rua das Estalagens** away from the market square. This street used to be filled with arts and crafts workshops, but in recent years it has gone upmarket with electronics, watch and jewellery shops, and boutiques. A few old relics remain, like the song bird shop at the corner of Estalagens and Travessa do Pagode, with its delicate wooden cages and other accessories.

Walk one block east and turn right into the Travessa do Pagode. Walk two blocks south and turn left into Rua de Madeira with its traditional woodwork shops. Rua de Madeira ends after a block, but cross over Rua Camilo Pessanha and enter a small alley called **Beco de Caixas**. If you are into old streets with lots of atmosphere, this is the best one in Macau. Walking along Caixas is like stepping into the Middle Ages. It is dark and smelly, lined with tiny shops and stalls selling live chickens and ducks, fresh fruit and vegetables, dried seafood products and century eggs. There is even a small Chinese shrine where the local merchants make offerings.

Caixas ends at Rua Mercadores. You can end the tour here by walking straight ahead, back to Largo do Senado. Or you can turn right on Mercadores and explore another old neighborhood on the south side of Avenida Almeida Ribeiro. Once you cross the busy avenue, the street is called Travessa Aterro Novo. Walk straight ahead to **Rua Felicidade** and turn right. This used to be the red light district of Macau, but nowadays Felicidade is known for its many restaurants and cafes. In fact, this is the single biggest collection of eating places in the entire city. One of the better-known eating places is **Fat Siu Lau** (Laughing Buddha) at the corner of Felicidade and Travessa da Mastro, which opened more than 90 years ago as the first European-style restaurant in Macau.

Rua Felicidade and its continuation, Rua Caldeira, end at the waterfront, skirting behind the old **Kam Pek Casino**. All the cross streets that run off to the right lead back to Avenida Almeida Ribeiro and the city centre.

Afternoon Itineraries

3. Three Colinas

Walk up three prominent hills for great views of Macau, visit the oldest lighthouse on the China coast and the 17th-century Kun Iam Tong, Macau's largest Buddhist sanctuary.

This strenuous afternoon walk takes in three of Macau's more prominent hills: Colina da Guia, Montanha Russa and Colina de Mong-Ha, each with its own unique views of the peninsula and surrounding waters.

Walk or have a taxi drop you off at the top of **Colina da Guia** which rises 99m (325ft), the highest point in peninsular Macau. **Guia Lighthouse** (daily 9am–5.30pm) is one of the most prominent landmarks in the Portuguese colony. Built in 1865, the squat white tower is the oldest lighthouse on the China coast. Originally lit with paraffin oil from the Middle East, an electric beam replaced the old gas lamp in 1909. The light shines bright each night, reaching as far as 32km (20 miles) across the Pearl River Estuary. Next to the lighthouse is a solid steel pole where typhoon signals are hoisted. The nearby guardhouse has been transformed into a small cafe.

Guia Lighthouse

Surrounding the lighthouse are the remains of **Guia Fort**, a small bastion (completed in 1638) used primarily as an observation post by Portuguese forces. Two of the original brick turrets remain, as does the **Chapel of Our Lady of Guia**. According to local legend, an image of the Virgin Mary appeared on this hill during a battle with the Dutch in 1622 and she raised her cloak to deflect enemy bullets. After their victory the Portuguese built this chapel in her honour. The chapel is open once a year, on August 5th, the feast day of Our Lady of Guia. Inside the chapel are a modest altar, a portrait of John the Baptist and the remains of frescoes that once covered the walls and ceiling of the chapel.

A leafy path called the **Estrada do Engenheiro Trigo** starts from the lower parking lot below the lighthouse, looping around the summit of Colina da Guia through one of the largest parks in the city. The park has a 2-km (1¼-mile) long trail and fitness circuit with 20 exercise stations.

Flora Gardens

Exit by **Flora Gardens** on the northwest face. Two steep trails lead downhill past a large aviary filled with native birds. The gardens take their name from Flora Palace, a colonial villa that was burnt down in the 1920s after an explosion at the adjacent firecracker factory. All that remains is the foundation, which has been converted into a small zoo with dingy cages holding monkeys, turtles, birds and a rather melancholy Himalayan black bear.

Leave the gardens and turn right into the busy Avenida Sidonio Pais. Cross Avenida do Coronel Mesquita and walk up a narrow street called Estrada Ferreira do Amaral. At the top of the street is the lovely **Montanha Russa Garden**, one of the city's most tranquil confines. The entrance is on the south side, next to a statue of St

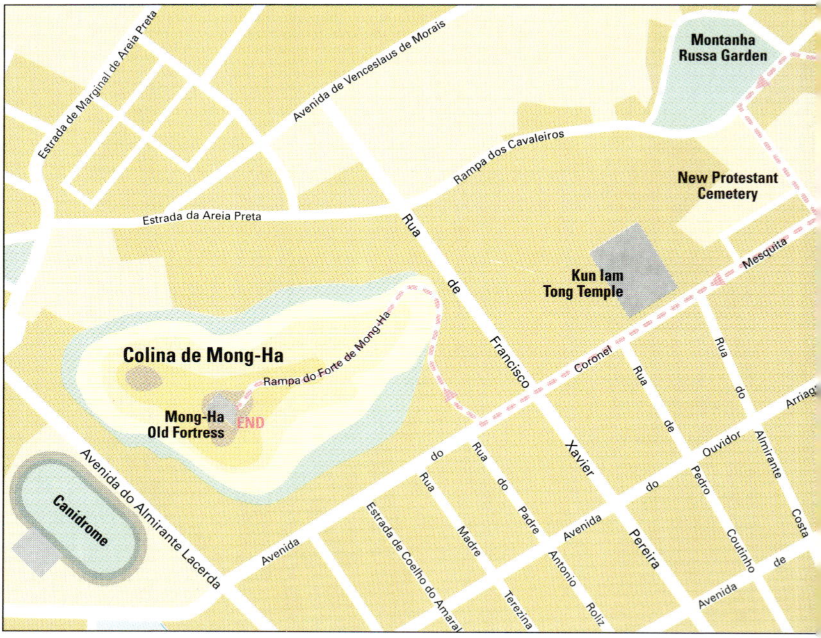

John Bosco. The gardens feature a mix of lush tropical and temperate vegetation, with impressive palms and huge camphor trees. A trail spirals to the top of **Russa Hill** with views of the adjacent cemetery and power station. Until a few years ago you could peer across the border into China, but the panorama is blocked by massive apartment blocks in the northern part of the city.

Montanha Russa Cafe (Tel: 302731) is a great place to linger over a glass of wine, or lunch if you have not eaten yet. The outdoor tables are popular with Portuguese bureaucrats and businessmen who come for the beef steaks, cod and African chicken.

Head down the Rua Silva Mendes past the outer wall of the New Protestant Cemetery and turn right into Avenida do Coronel Mesquita. Walk down to the **Kun Iam Tong Temple** (daily 7am–6pm), the colony's largest Buddhist sanctuary on your right. The present temple was founded in the early 17th century, during the Ming Dynasty, on land outside the Portuguese walls. But there may have been a place of worship on this site since the 13th century. The main building consists of three altars, each on a slightly higher level, with stone walls and wooden roofs smothered in intricate carvings. Within are three golden Buddhas, a statue of Kun Iam (the Goddess of Mercy) and figures of the 18 *Luohan* (Wisemen).

Luxuriant gardens and pavilions surround the temple. A round stone table in a courtyard marks where the Viceroy of Canton and American diplomat Caleb Cushing penned a friendship treaty between China and the United States in 1844. Further along is a celebrated

Smouldering joss stick at Kun Iam Tong Temple

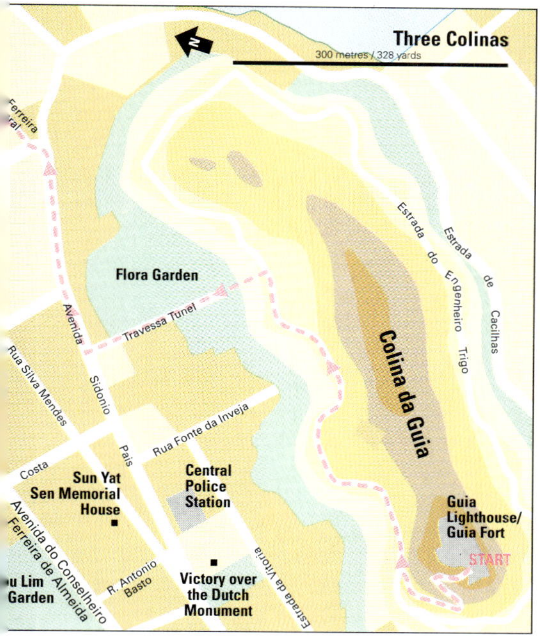

'lovers' tree'. According to legend, the four banyans fused after two young lovers committed suicide beneath the branches because their families disapproved of their romance.

From the temple, walk west to the junction of the Rua de Francisco Xavier Pereira. Cross it and continue a block to the entrance of a twisting lane on the right.

This lane leads to the top of **Colina de Mong-Ha**. Crowning the summit is a brick-and-concrete bastion, **Mong-Ha Fort**, commissioned in 1849 to stop a Chinese invasion that never happened. Now dilapidated and overgrown with weeds, the Mong-Ha fort is much less impressive than the other city strongholds. Still, the ramparts offer interesting views of the Inner Harbour, Ilha Verde (Green Island) at the north end of the harbour, and the **Canidrome** dog-racing track below.

Below the entrance gate is a cluster of old military buildings that have been taken over by the Macau Government Tourist Office (MGTO) for use as a hotel training school and a diplomatic guesthouse called the **Pousada Mong-Ha**. The restaurant is open to the public on Friday evenings, when students prepare a sumptuous Macanese buffet (dinner: 7–9.30pm). Reservations should be made one day in advance (Tel: 561252).

Take a taxi back into downtown Macau, or catch a bus from the intersection of Avenida Mesquita and Rua de Francisco Xavier Pereira. Buses No 12, 18 and 28C stop near the Lisboa Hotel.

4. Coloane Beachcomber

A relaxed afternoon at Hac Sa and Cheoc Van beaches along the south shore of Coloane Island.

You can spend the morning hiking around **Alto Coloane** mountain before you hit the beach. Or head straight for the sand by Moke, taxi or public bus No 21A (from outside the Lisboa Hotel) which stops at both Cheoc Van and Hac Sa.

Hac Sa (Black Sand) **Beach** is the colony's favourite weekend

Cheoc Van Beach

recreation spot, but it is usually deserted on weekdays. The big attraction is a black sand beach that curves around the bay in a swarthy crescent. The water is often tinted brown from silt carried down from central China by the Pearl River, but otherwise Hac Sa is considered one of the cleanest beaches in the region.

There is usually a brisk wind blowing in off the South China Sea, which means that Hac Sa Bay is perfect for windsurfing and sailing. Several sheds along the shore rent water sports equipment. They are open daily in summer and on weekends only for the rest of the year.

Behind the beach is a grove of trees with food stalls, cafes and the Hac Sa sports and recreation complex. **Fernando's Restaurant** has been a Macau landmark for more than a decade, with some of the best Portuguese seafood this side of Lisbon. The white beans, sardines and squid are especially tasty. You can also cook your own food along the beach: the cafe to the left of Fernando's sells barbecue charcoal and skewers.

The **sports complex** (daily 9am–10pm) is a private facility run by Clube Solaqua. It has an Olympic-sized swimming pool, roller-skating rink, model airplane field, soccer pitch, miniature golf course and playground. The pool is open to the general public. Directly behind the complex is the **Macau Riding Centre**, where horses can be hired for a ride along the beach.

Hac Sa's newest attraction is the **Westin Resort**, a luxury hotel and sports complex set on a rocky headland on the north side of the beach. With brick-coloured walls set amidst lush tropical landscape, it is likely to conjure up images of Acapulco or Ibiza rather than China. The Westin is adjacent to the new **Macau Golf and Country Club**, which has the colony's only grass tennis courts and golf links, an 18-hole championship course where the Macau Open will be played in future years. At present, the course is open to club members and Westin hotel guests only.

If Hac Sa is not enough to keep you busy for the afternoon, head for **Cheoc Van Beach**. Because the strand faces the South China Sea directly, the water here tends to be rougher than at Hac Sa. Bus No 21A plies between the two beaches. Cheoc Van has a boat club which rents windsurfing boards, sailboats and canoes to the public. Nearby is a public swimming pool with a restaurant, bar and changing rooms. And on the hill behind the boat club is the **Pousada de Coloane**, a popular weekend hotel for people from Hong Kong. Its restaurant is well-known for its Sunday buffet, but Portuguese and Brazilian dishes are available throughout the week.

5. Penha Peninsula

A figure-eight walk along the crest of the Penha Peninsula including Penha Church, Santa Sancha and the Bela Vista Hotel.

This itinerary starts in front of **St Lawrence's Church** at the intersection of Rua de Sao Lourenco and Travessa Padre Narciso. Walk south along a narrow street called Rua Padre Antonio, hemmed in by typical middle-class apartment buildings with shops on the ground floor.

Turn left into the Rua Penha and proceed up the hill, past an abandoned convent school called Bom Jesus. You will soon reach a junction where five streets come together. Straight ahead is the famed Bela Vista Hotel, but turn right at this point and scale a steep cobblestoned street called **Calcada de Penha** which offers some fine views of the Inner Harbour as well as mainland China.

At the top of the street is **Penha Church** (daily 10am–4pm), one of Macau's most notable landmarks and highest points. The first church on this site was built in 1622 by Portuguese sailors who survived a close call with an invading Dutch fleet. It became a place of pilgrimage and prayer for sailors embarking on dangerous journeys. The church was rebuilt in 1837 and then again in 1935 along its present lines. The terrace outside offers superb views of the Praia Grande

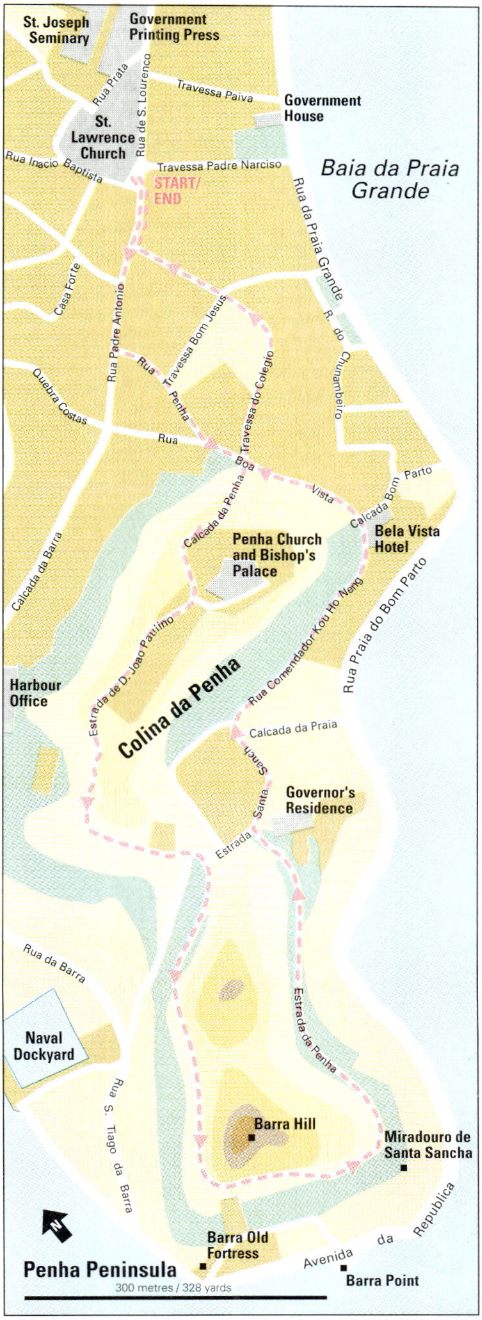

Penha Church, one of Macau's highest points

and Outer Harbour. You can look straight down on Santa Sancha, the Macau Governor's residence, from here.

The dark and imposing **Bishop's Palace** (built in 1837) sits behind the church, on the site of **Penha Fort**, a Portuguese bastion that once formed part of the protective cordon around Macau. The building is home to the Archbishop of Macau, spiritual head of the territory's 30,000 Roman Catholics.

Exit the church grounds and walk along the twisting Estrada de Joao Paulino, which skirts the western edge of Colina da Penha. After about five minutes you come to a junction where five streets come together in front of a small park. Take the second street on the right, Estrada da Penha, which curls around the summit of Barra Hill to this same junction.

By night, **Estrada da Penha** is a Lovers' Lane for young couples. But during the day it offers unsurpassed views of the Outer and Inner Harbours and the islands beyond. The street also boasts of some of the most expensive properties in Macau, modern luxury villas and condos that sprawl down the mountainside. At the southern end of the loop is a small park called **Miradouro de Santa Sancha** with benches, shady trees and a view across the water to Taipa.

The loop eventually swings around to the front of **Santa Sancha**, the governor's mansion. The villa is not open to the public, but you can gaze through the wrought iron gates at its pink-and-white facade, with louvred wooden window shutters, balustrades and stucco trim. Built in the 1840s, Santa Sancha was commissioned by a prominent Macanese family and designed by local architect Jose Agostinho de Aquino, who also conceived St Lawrence's Church and Government House. The mansion remained in private hands until 1923 when it was sold to the government. Next door is the Military Tennis Club.

Bela Vista Hotel

Next, you should follow Estrada Santa Sancha and Rua Comendador Kou Ho Neng in an eastwardly direction to the **Bela Vista Hotel**, one of the grand old dames of the China coast. The original hotel (called the Boa

Vista) was opened in 1880s by an English sea captain who thought he could draw affluent holidaymakers from Hong Kong. But the scheme failed, and the hotel was forced to close its doors around the turn of the century. Over the next 50 years, the building was used as a school, World War II refugee centre and British military club. It was re-christened a hotel in 1950 and this time the Bela Vista became popular with the Hong Kong crowd.

In the late 1980s, the Macau government purchased the property and contracted Hong Kong's Mandarin Oriental Group to transform it into a luxury boutique hotel. The result is stunning: one of the most romantic (and expensive) places to stay in Asia. Even if you do not stay overnight, have a drink in the bar, or lunch on the verandah with its panoramic views of Macau and the harbour.

If you can manage to pry yourself away from the bar, follow Rua Boa Vista, Travessa do Colegio and Calcada da Paz to your starting point in front of St Lawrence's Church.

Evening Itineraries

6. Cabaret Evening

A wild night on the town: Asia's most acclaimed nude revue, the Crazy Paris show; followed by discos, hostess clubs and ending with a late night massage.

Macau has more nightlife than just about any other city in Asia. And it is not just gambling. There is a vast array of after-dark enterprises from bars, cafes and musical revues, to more iniquitous establishments like hostess clubs and massage parlours. These tours, to be done by taxi or private car, are designed to give you as much variety as you can fit into a single evening.

Start with the happy hour(5–7pm) at **The Bar** (Tel: 831234) in the Hyatt Regency Hotel in Taipa, where you can get two drinks for the price of one.

Next, move on to the legendary **Crazy Paris** show at the Lisboa Hotel, the most acclaimed nude revue in Asia. A dozen gorgeous dancers strut their stuff, and yes, they take it all off. But it is hard to call the show raunchy, because the girls are clothed 90 percent of the time in lavish costumes for song and dance routines devised by the resident French choreographer. You might have a Parisian can-can, an Argentine rope dance, a Madonna-like disco frenzy or something strictly leather.

The girls are mostly European and American; the audience is largely Asian, especially Taiwanese and mainland Chinese tourists who find the show (daily 8pm, 9.30pm; Saturday, extra show at 11pm) quite risque. The early show is recommended because it gives you more time for the rest of this itinerary. By the time you leave Crazy Paris it should be around 9pm. Take an hour for dinner at any of the excellent restaurants in the downtown area. Then, head back to the waterfront, to the **Skylight Disco** (Tel: 553888) in the Presidente Hotel. The club offers a superb view of the Outer Harbour. But you will probably be looking the other way, at the Skylight floorshow, a less flamboyant version of the Crazy Paris show. Stay and dance at Skylight, or head uptown to **Mondial Disco** (Tel: 566866) on Rua da Antonio Basto.

The Mondial is where young Portuguese and Macanese hang out on Friday and Saturday night. There's a good mix of bureaucrats, students and businessmen, and the overall ambience is very European – this could easily be a Lisbon club. The music ranges from contemporary European techno-pop and funk to American rap and house, with a few Top 40 numbers thrown in for good measure. For a quiet interlude, head for the **Bar da Guia** (Tel: 587888) in the Mandarin Oriental Hotel. Macau habitues consider this the city's most elegant watering hole, with its sweeping harbour view and a resident Filipino band.

You can call it a night at this point, or move on to the other side of midnight, into the more ambiguous nightlife sectors: **hostess clubs** and **massage parlours**. The Japanese invented hostess clubs in the early 1980s as an updated version of geisha entertainment, and the concept quickly spread through the rest of Asia. The idea is to create an atmosphere where a man can relax in the company of a woman who is not his wife or girlfriend. You can talk, drink and dance at a rate of around Ptc 2.50 per minute. But you cannot take the girl back to your hotel unless you 'buy' her from the club for a steep fee. What you and your hostess do later is your business, but be prepared to pay again. The minimum charge at most clubs is Ptc 200 (US$25) but you could end up paying as much as US$500. Macau's hostess clubs are concentrated in the Si Toi Building on Rua Praia da Grande, one block east of Avenida Almeida Ribeiro. There are many Thai restaurants in this area because many of the working girls are Thai. There are numerous clubs to choose from, but the biggest is **Tonnochy Nightclub** with over 180 girls, a live band and private karaoke rooms available on request.

Among the other established hostess clubs are **China City** (Tel: 312333) in the old Jai Alai fronton on Avenida Amizade near the ferry terminal, and **Club de Savoy** (Tel: 332222) in the Lisboa Hotel. One of the newer players is the **Metropolitan** (Tel: 831111) in the New Century Hotel on Taipa Island, which has just about everything you need for a night's entertainment: a hundred gorgeous girls, karaoke rooms, strip show and live Filipino band.

Sauna and massage are other late-night options. Once again, you can play it straight or ask for extra special service.

The Si Toi Building has a number of outlets including **Sauna Mona Lisa** (Tel: 565888) and **Sauna Volvo** (Tel: 558877). Further afield are **Darling Thai Massage and Sauna** (Tel: 337733) in the Jai Alai building and **Centro Sauna Massage** (Tel: 593553) at 72 Avenida Ferreira de Almeida. For a legitimate massage or sauna, there is **Lisboa Hotel Health Spa** which has separate sections for males (Tel: 593888) and females (Tel: 345333), open until 7am.

7. The Ultimate Casino Crawl

Join in the stakes or watch others do so at casinos, the dog-racing tracks or the Macau Jockey Club.

How much gambling can you cram into a single evening? Find out by taking the ultimate casino crawl around Macau.

This tour works only on Tuesday, Thursday, Saturday and Sunday when there is dog racing, or on the occasional Wednesday evening when there are pony races.

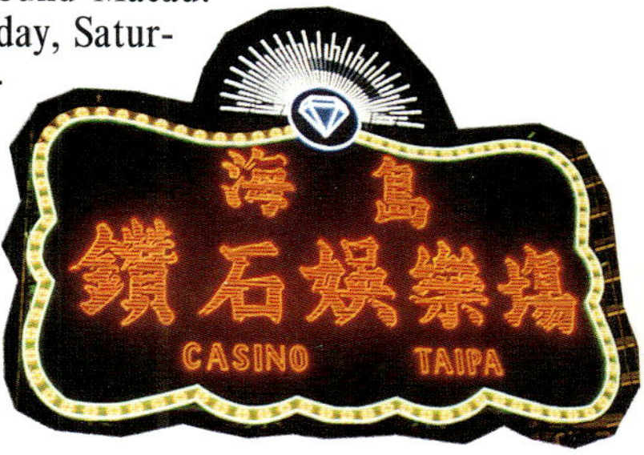

Start with the greyhound races at the **Canidrome** at 8pm (Tel: 574413; Entrance fee: Ptc 5, minimum bet: Ptc 5) in northern Macau, near the Chinese border. The dogs come from professional kennels in Australia, America and the British Isles. There are normally 14 races on the card. Odds and winnings are displayed on a huge matrix screen in the infield; the betting is completely computerized. The place is usually packed with Hong Kong punters taking a break from the races at Shatin and Happy Valley.

Or, you can start the evening at the **Macau Jockey Club** (Tel: 321888; Entrance fee: Ptc 20 for non-members, minimum bet: Ptc 10) on Taipa Island at 7.15pm (Twilight events start at 3:30pm). There are all sorts of betting combinations: Quinellas, trifectas and double-quinellas. The ponies normally race around a grass oval, but many of the evening meets are run on sand (the race track, by the way, doubled as Macau's airport back in the days when everyone travelled on small fixed-wing aircraft). The 18,000-seat grandstand features luxury boxes, restaurants and its own indoor gambling hall, the **Victoria Casino** (Tel: 321888).

After the last race, you have the whole night to bet the rest of your money. The closest casino to the dogs is the **Jai Alai** (Tel: 726129) in the old jai alai arena near the ferry terminal. From there, work your way down the waterfront with stops at the **Mandarin Oriental** (Tel 567888), **Kingsway** (Tel: 702888) and **Lisboa** (Tel: 577666). Alternatively, try the older, Asian-style casinos of the Inner Harbour: the **Macau Palace** floating casino and the **Kam Pek**. From the Macau Jockey Club it is only a short taxi ride to the **Taipa Casino** in the Hyatt Regency Hotel. (See the *Nightlife* section.)

8. Zhuhai and Zhongshan Hot Springs

A day-long tour of the Zhuhai Special Economic Zone and the nearby Zhongshan Hot Springs, with a stop at the Sun Yat-sen House in Cuiheng.

Get a Macau travel agent to arrange visas and transport for this excursion to Southern China. Generally, guided tours in air-conditioned minibuses cost Ptc 270–320 (HK$260–310). The cost includes visa and lunch.

Guangdong Province in southern China is the heartland of Cantonese language and culture. For several thousand years, it nurtured a prosperous mercantile economy. But the Communist Revolution ended this and kept Guangdong in the dark for the better part of 40 years. Economic reforms in the last decade have ushered in a new era of capitalism and prosperity. In fact, the province had the world's fastest economic growth rate in the early 1990s.

Within Guangdong, one of the fastest growing areas is **Zhuhai Special Economic Zone** (SEZ), across the border from Macau. The SEZs were established by the communist government in the early 1980s as a means to stimulate rapid economic growth in certain coastal areas without rocking socialism in the rest of China. They have succeeded beyond the wildest dreams of the bureaucrats who put them in place. A decade ago, Zhuhai was a sleepy coastal area with about 100,000 people. Today, it is a thriving factory town, with a population of more than 600,000 and a rapidly expanding middle class who drive Japanese cars, watch Hong Kong television and slip across the border to gamble in Macau.

The town directly across the border from Macau is called **Gongbei**. But there

Yung Mak Village

really is little to see except for flashy new skyscrapers like the Yindo Hotel and bustling joint-venture factories where companies like Canon and Mitsumi make consumer electronics for export. Rural China (in the form of Zhongshan County) starts beyond the Zhuhai SEZ border post, with rice paddies and rustic villages stretching into the horizon.

From Gongbei, it is another 18km (11¼ miles) to **Yung Mak**, a small town in Zhongshan County. A model tourist village replete with shops and home tours, Yung Mak may not be the 'real' China, but it does offer a glimpse of modern life behind the Bamboo Curtain. Yung Mak's real claim to fame lies in the fact that American pop icon Michael Jackson came here in 1987 on a brief tour of southern China. A photo of Jackson and a local baby appears in *Moonwalker*, his autobiography, and you can find photos of the singer displayed next to images of Buddha and Chairman Mao in village homes. Local craftsmen sell embroidered tablecloths for about a quarter of the price you would pay in Hong Kong.

Travel another five minutes, or less than 1km (½ mile) via the Sanxiang-Xiazha Road to the **Zhongshan Hot Springs**. The hot springs are a local attempt to cash in on the golf craze sweeping Asia. There are thermal baths here, but the foremost attraction is an 18-hole golf course designed by Arnold Palmer, one of the best in China. A second course, designed by Jack Nicklaus, is on the way. The course draws mobs of Western and Chinese businessmen from Hong Kong, who arrive via direct ferry services at Zhuhai City. Green fees run into HK$450–600 depending on the time of week. Caddies and clubs are available for hire for another HK$200.

Zhongshan Hot Springs

Facilities include tennis courts, stables, Chinese and Western restaurants, naturally-heated pools and a shooting range where you can test your luck with an AK-47 assault rifle. You can lunch at the hot springs' restaurants or at the Cuiheng Hotel, opposite the Sun Yat-sen Museum in Cuiheng city, your next destination.

About 16km (10 miles) northeast of the hot springs in Zhongshan County is a small city called **Cuiheng**, birthplace of Dr Sun Yat-sen, who led the 1911 Revolution that overthrew the Manchu (Qing) Dynasty. His memory is kept alive at several locations.

The **Sun Yat-sen Home** is in pristine condition. Much of the original lycheewood furniture remains, as do many family mementoes, like a paraffin lamp that Dr Sun brought back from his exile in Hawaii, his stethoscope, globe, ink slab, and jars in which he stored explosives. Born here in 1866, Dr Sun lived here again in the 1890s while plotting the 1911 Revolution.

Sun Yat-sen Museum

Behind the house is the new **Sun Yat-sen Museum**, a misnomer, because the collection reflects life in rural Guangdong Province rather than anything about the revolutionary leader. The museum is built around the concept of a typical Cantonese village, with houses devoted to merchants, peasants, fishermen and people from other walks of life. There is also a fine gift shop where you can buy custom-made stone and jade seals, calligraphy scrolls, jade animal figures, paper lanterns and other souvenirs.

Within walking distance of the house/museum compound is **Sun Yat-sen Memorial High School** where some of the best young minds in China study. Feel free to wander around the grounds; the students and teachers are quite friendly and always willing to talk to foreigners. Look out for the student 'newspaper' – outdoor chalkboards on which students write about current events in Chinese characters. The school also has its own shop, specialising in the works of Wuhan-based artist He Guan Zhi.

It is 30km (18¾ miles) back to Macau along the new coast road,

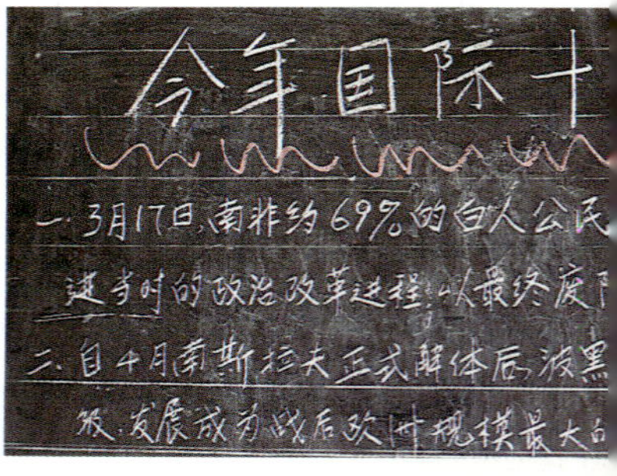

'Newspapers' at the Sun Yat-sen school

a four-lane expressway that will one day connect Macau and Guangzhou. The highway runs past the **Pearl Land** amusement park, a Chinese version of Magic Mountain with three roller-coasters, ferris wheel and other thrill rides. The HK$20 entry fee includes tickets for five rides. Next door is the **Zhuhai Country Club**, the other big golf club in the region. The highway continues through the middle of Zhuhai City with its towering apartment blocks and department stores.

9. Guangzhou (Canton)

An overnight trip to Guangzhou, visiting the Temple of the Six Banyans, Yuexiu Park and the beautiful 14th-century Ming Dynasty palace, Zhenhai Tower.

Guangzhou (Canton) is a huge city at the top of the Pearl River Delta, the capital of Guangdong province, the metropolis of southern China and the largest Cantonese-speaking city in the world after Hong Kong. Transport links with Macau are tenuous at the present time. Travelling by public buses or private car is not recommended but there is an overnight (6pm–7am) ferry service from Macau to Guangzhou. Tickets are sold at Yuet Tong Ltd offices at the Inner Harbour. Package tours are also available from travel agents in Macau. For those with the stamina, Guangzhou makes a fascinating side trip.

The population hovers around 3½ million, but there could easily be a million more given the massive influx of people from the countryside in recent years, searching for their slice of the booming Guangzhou economy. The city has been a great trading centre for more than 1,000 years, and this is where the Europeans merchants gained their foothold on trade in China.

From Zhoutouzui Wharf, walk across the Renmin Bridge to **Shamian Island** in the Pearl River. For nearly 100 years, this was a European trading 'factory'. The British and French shared its administration until World War II and they left their architecture behind in the form of stately mansions and churches. There are outdoor cafes and pleasant waterfront promenades and towering over everything is the luxurious **White Swan Hotel** with its indoor waterfall and magnificent views of the river.

Cross the bridge back to the mainland and take bus No 3 near the intersection of Liu'ersan Lu ('Lu' means 'road' in Mandarin) and Remin Nanlu. Ask the driver to let you off at the intersection of Zhongshan Lu and Liurong Lu. Walk for about five minutes' north along Liurong Lu to the **Temple of the Six Banyans** (Liurong Temple), the city's foremost centre of Buddhism. There has been a place of worship here for more than 1,400 years. And there are actually six banyans, immortalized by Su Dongpo, a famous Sung Dynasty poet. The hub of the complex is the **Flowery Pagoda** which rises 60m (187ft) above the surrounding gardens. A spiral staircase leads to the top floor. Behind the pagoda is a large wooden pavilion with three giant gold Buddhas.

The statues were boarded up during the Cultural Revolution and not exposed again until the early 1980s. Buddhist monks and nuns live in the outlying buildings. Nearby is another exquisite structure, **Guangxiao Temple**, surrounded by tranquil gardens and rarely visited by tourists.

Retrace your steps to Zhongshan Lu, reboard the No 3 bus heading north and alight at the China (Zhongguo) Hotel. **Yuexiu Park** is on the east side of the Jiefang Beilu. It is a huge green space in the middle of the city, with wooded hills, meadows and lakes. As the ram is a symbol of Guangzhou, the highest hill is crowned by a famous **Statue of the Five Rams** where Chinese tourists have their picture taken. Nearby is the 14th-century **Zhenhai Tower**, a beautiful Ming Dynasty palace that houses the **City Museum**. Inside are exhibits and artifacts related to Guangzhou history.

On the south side of the park is **Sun Yat-sen Memorial Hall**, a performance venue and the most handsome building in the city. The blue-glazed roof is reminiscent of the Temple of Heaven in Peking.

Golden Buddhas in Liurong Temple

Have a Cantonese *dim sum* lunch at the very old **Beiyuan** restaurant (No 318 Xiao Bei Lu, Tel: 33365) near the western edge of Yuexiu Park before moving on. Ask for a table upstairs where you can look down on the hustle and bustle in the main dining room.

In the western part of Guangzhou, near the intersection of Liwan Lu and Zhongshan Lu (about 30 minutes' walk or a 10-minute bike ride from the Sun Yat-sen Memorial Hall) is the **Chen Family Temple**. The temple is quite modern by Chinese standards, with intricately carved wooden beams and glazed pottery sculptures; it was built in the 1890s with donations from Chen clan organizations all over south China. Its two main functions were worship and education. Nowadays, the complex is a government museum and arts complex. Ceramics and bonsai trees are on sale.

To round off the day, have dinner at the **Panxi Restaurant** (No 151 Longjin Xi Lu, Tel: 89318/85655). One of the oldest eating houses in southern China, it has a dozen pavilions spread across several islands in a small lake. The pavilions are connected to each other by quaint wooden bridges.

The 14th century Zhenhai Tower is now a museum

Shopping

Macau, though less well-known than Hong Kong for its shopping, is an even better shopping destination in some respects. Like Hong Kong, the colony is a duty-free port. Unlike Hong Kong, its vendors tend to be friendlier. Overheads are also lower in Macau – resulting in a nicer shopping environment and generally lower prices.

Many vendors expect you to bargain. So when in doubt, ask for their 'best price' and see if they are willing to negotiate. As elsewhere, be sure to get a proper receipt and a warranty card for expensive items.

Fashion

Many world-famous labels have their garments manufactured in Macau, so over-runs and seconds find their way into the street markets at incredible prices. To counteract this, some companies (like Benetton and Crocodile) have opened their own boutiques which offer branded merchandise at prices well below their stores abroad. Crocodile's boutique is near the corner of Avenida Almeida Ribeiro and Rua de Cinco Outuburo while Benetton's is on the same street, west of Leal Senado. Bossini also has a boutique at No 61, Avenida Infante de Henrique.

St Dominic's market

St Dominic's Market is full of clothing stalls, as are Rua da Palha near the ruins of St Paul's and Rua Cinco de Outubro near the Inner Harbour. Look out for denim wear, T-shirts, cotton sports clothes, children's wear.

Gold, Jewellery & Gemstones

Macau has been famous for its gold since World War II when it became a haven for the metal smuggled out of China. Since then, gold

Camphor chests, Rua Da Tercena

has blossomed into a major local passion. Prices are so low that even Hong Kong residents come across to buy. Jewellery stores and pawnshops near the casinos are packed with rings, necklaces and bangles set with pearls, diamonds, emerald, rubies, sapphires, opals and other precious stones. You can find traditional and contemporary designs, and if you are staying a few days you can order custom-made pieces.

As pure gold is a popular form of investment for local Chinese, most jewellers also sell 24-carat items and gold bars by weight (plus a small mark-up for workmanship).

The jewellers and pawnshops are concentrated mainly along the following areas: Avenida Infante D Henrique between Sintra Square and Leal do Senado; Rua da Escola Commercial behind the Lisboa Hotel; Rua Caldeira behind Kam Pek Casino; and Rua das Estalagens in the Tercena District.

Antiques

If you know antiques, you might find a good buy around the dark lanes off Rua das Estalagens and Travessa Pagode. If you don't, stick to reputable stores along Rua da Tercena. The days are gone when you could find treasures at bargain prices. But you can still get genuine articles if you are prepared to pay for them.

Flea market vendor

Porcelain at Rua-Sao Paolo

Look out for: Ming and Ching dishes, vases and stools; antique jewellery; porcelain and jade figurines; rosewood and blackwood furniture; camphor chests; embroidered screens; old Macanese, Portuguese and Chinese currency, and stamps.

Every afternoon, a flea market is set up at the intersection of Rua da Tercena and Rua Nossa Senhora do Amparo. It is mostly filled with junk but you can also find stamps, coins and paper money, pieces of jade, odds and ends of porcelain, wooden abacus sets and small Buddha figurines. Look for an interesting street stall with old stamps, coins and paper money at the corner of Avenida Almeida Ribeiro and Travessa do Matadouro.

Handicrafts & Furniture

Macau's handicrafts are mainly Chinese in nature. There is a staggering array of beautiful porcelain tableware, vases, bowls and flower pots in both traditional and contemporary designs along

Rattan furniture shop

Rua Sao Paulo and Travessa dos Algibebes to the left of the steps leading up to St Paul's. Rua da Tercena is famous for its furniture shops – chests, benches, chairs and tables – intricately carved and inlaid with mother-of-pearl or marble.

There is a shop selling beautifully-crafted wooden bird cages and song birds at the corner of Rua das Estalagens and Travessa Pagode. The stalls at the bottom of the steps leading up to St Paul's offer an array of knick-knacks, as well as Mao buttons and hats from China. And an interesting few hours can also be spent scouting the shops that sell sweet-smelling joss sticks and incense coils, family alters and paper offerings in the form of money, television sets and videos, mobile phones and even luxury cars – anything one may need in the afterlife.

Traditional Herbs & Foods

Even if you are at the peak of health, you must not miss a visit to a traditional Chinese medicinal store where you will find strange-looking plants, roots, fungi and animal parts on display in glass cases and jars. The medicine men will make up a prescription for whatever ails you and then calculate the bill at breakneck speed on a wooden abacus. There is a marvellous old Chinese pharmacy on Rua Camilo Pessanha near the Inner Harbour. It has glass jars full of preserved animal and vegetable parts, display cases of deer antlers, tiger penises, ginseng roots and lizards on sticks.

Dried foodstuff stores also open up a whole new world. The merchandise is normally sold from large wooden bins – dried mushrooms, plums, ginseng, sharks fin, abalone, seahorses and more. Rua das Lorchas and the western end of Avenida Almeida Ribeiro have a number of dried food outlets. Shops at the south end of Rua de Cinco Outubro (between Ribeiro and Lorchas) specialise in spicy barbecue-dried meat, similar in taste and texture to beef jerky.

Supermarkets, Department Stores, Drugs & Spirits

There are several Park'N Shop supermarkets in Macau, including a branch at No 69 Avenida de Sidonio Pais near the Sun Yat-sen House. The store stocks a large variety of both Western and Chinese food items.

Macau's first big department store is Yaohan (daily 11am–11pm), opposite the ferry terminal, with 5,520sq m (60,000sq ft) of display space. Yaohan also has a supermarket and bakery, as well as a McDonald's outlet.

Watson's (daily 10am–10pm) dispenses a wide selection of international brand toiletries and drugs from a branch at the corner of Rua Santa Clara and Rua do Campo.

Portuguese wine and port is duty-free in Macau and often cheaper than in Europe. Hong Heng liquor store at 61 Avenida Infante D Henrique has a large selection.

Eating Out

Many people say that you can trace the heritage of the Portuguese empire in native Macanese food. By the time the Portuguese arrived in China, they had already picked up culinary tips from their colonies in South America, Africa and India – which they mixed with innate homeland influences and Chinese ingredients to create Macanese cuisine.

This explains dishes that seem out of place in the Orient: spicy African chicken; *feijoada*, a Brazilian stew made from pork, sausage and beans; *matapa*, a blend of spinach, saffron and giant prawns that came from Angola, and the ubiquitous *bacalhau* – grilled, boiled, stewed and fried cod – plus sardines and thick, country-style soups from Iberia.

The origin of other Macanese dishes cannot be traced to a single country. *Minchi* is a combination of pork and potatoes fried in soya sauce. *Galinha a Portuguesa* comprises chicken, olives, egg and potatoes baked in olive oil with coconut, tomato, saffron and curry seasoning – a recipe that is completely alien to the motherland.

Macau is also a great place for Chinese food, with restaurants specializing in dishes from several regions. Teochew and Shanghainese restaurants are popular, but the majority are Cantonese, offering shark's fin soup, fresh vegetables, spring rolls and delicious *dim sum* delicacies.

In recent years, restaurants from the rest of the whole world are finding a ready clientele in Macau: Japanese, Korean, Thai, Vietnamese, Indian, Burmese, African, Italian and American. One thing most restaurants have in common is an extensive cellar of inexpensive Portuguese wine, brandies and port.

A rough guide for a three-course

Macanese food has many origins

dinner for one person excluding beverages, tax and tips is as follows:
Expensive = above HK$40
Moderate = HK$28–HK$40
Inexpensive = under HK$28.

Portuguese/Macanese

A Galera
Hotel Lisboa,
Avenida da Amizade
Tel: 577666, ext 1152
This elegantly decorated grill room has surprisingly reasonable prices. The home-made soups are delicious, as are the salted fish and the stuffed squid. Live music nightly. Open 12.30–2.30pm, 7–11pm. *Inexpensive*

A Lorcha
289 Rua do Almirante Sergio
Tel: 313193
The food is excellent, especially the casseroles, and the waterfront location is romantic. Open 1–3pm, 7–11pm. *Inexpensive*

Afonso's
Hyatt Regency Hotel,
No 2 Estonda Almirante Marques Esparteiro, Taipa
Tel: 831234, ext 1921
Excellent food in a formal setting, this is one of the places where Macau's politicians and bureaucrats take their distinguished visitors. There are various fish and meat entrees, or you can make a full meal by combining various starters like spicy crab soup, cod balls and green salad with olives and feta cheese. The wine list is extensive, but very reasonable. Half bottles of Portuguese wine start at Ptc 40. Open noon–3pm, 7–11pm. *Moderate*

Cacarola
No 8 Rua das Gaivotas, Coloane
Tel: 328226
A darling with local Portuguese because of its delicious Iberian cuisine, including old-time favourites like cod and African chicken. *Inexpensive*

Estrela Do Mar
Rua Carlos Eugenio,
Taipa Village
Tel: 320843
Restaurant – owner Joao da Silva came to Macau 35 years ago as a soldier and stayed on as a restaurateur. Specialties include Portuguese chicken, breaded pork-chops, cod with egg and onion. Ask for the menu of the day. *Inexpensive*

Fat Siu Lau
64 Rua da Felicidade
Tel: 573585, 573580
The 'Laughing Buddha' has been around since 1903, the oldest restaurant in Macau. As with many older restaurants, the service can be a bit brusque at times, but the food is quite good. It has survived largely due to its reputation for great roast pigeon, but the menu also includes grilled sardines, steak cooked in garlic and spices, African chicken, Portuguese chicken in a coconut sauce and an 85-year-old closely-guarded recipe for roast chicken. Open 11–1.30am. *Inexpensive*

Fernando's
Hac Sa Beach, Coloane
Tel: 328531, 328264
Portuguese food at its best in an atmosphere redolent of an Algarve cafe. Situated on Hac Sa Beach, there is nothing pretentious about the decor, but the cuisine is first rate. Try the white beans in olive oil, the grilled sardines or the fresh squid. Open noon–9.30pm. *Inexpensive*

Delicious Portuguese food

FORTALEZA
Pousada de Sao Tiago Hotel,
Avenida da Republica
Tel: 378111
The most elegant restaurant in Macau, set within the stout confines of a 17th-century fortress at the tip of Barra Point. The menu includes Portuguese, Macanese and Continental cuisine. *Expensive*

GALO
45 Rua dos Clerigos,
Taipa Village
Tel: 327423, 327318
Country-style Portuguese cooking in a traditional village setting. Try the cod salad, a Portuguese spicy chicken and rice dish called *pipis*, and chilli crabs. Open 11.30am–10.30pm. *Inexpensive*

MONTANHA RUSSA
Montanha Russa Garden,
Estrada Ferreira do Amaral
Tel: 302731
Portuguese businessmen and bureaucrats flock to this place at lunch for the hearty food and inexpensive wine. The menu includes fish, beef and chicken dishes, plus salads and desserts. A large carafe of red or white wine costs only Ptc 30. Sit under the towering banyan trees outside and watch Chinese men from the neighbourhood take their birds out for a 'walk' in the surrounding gardens. Open noon–10pm. *Inexpensive*

PINOCCHIO'S
4 Rua do Sol,
Taipa Village
Tel: 327128, 327328

One of the best places in Macau for roast quail and chilli crab. The roast suckling pig is another speciality, but it has to be ordered in advance. This is a highly informal, cafe-style restaurant which can get unbelievably crowded (and noisy) on weekends. Open noon–10pm. *Inexpensive*

Pousada De Coloane Restaurant
Pousada de Coloane Hotel
Praia de Cheoc Van, Coloane
Tel: 328144, 328143
Famous for its Sunday brunch, which features a massive spread of Portuguese dishes. *Inexpensive*

Restaurante Portugues
16 Rua do Campo
Tel: 375445
Home-style Portuguese cooking in an equally homely atmosphere. Good cod soup, roast or steamed pig knuckles, beef kebabs with black pepper. There is also inexpensive red wine to accompany your meal. Open 11–1am. *Inexpensive*

Riquexo
69 Avenida Sidonio Pais
Tel: 565655
Riquexo is like no other restaurant in Macau, or all of Asia for that matter. This self-service cafe offers truly home-cooked lunch: entrees are prepared in private kitchens and delivered to the restaurant each day. Soups, salads, desserts, beer and wine are also available. A bright, family atmosphere. Open 11am–3pm. *Inexpensive*

Chinese

Long Kei
7b Largo do Senado
Tel: 573970
A very popular Cantonese restaurant with a huge selection – 359 different dishes. The simply decorated Long Kei is noisy and busy. And you can't beat the location – right on Senado Square in the heart of the old town. Open 11.30am–11pm. *Inexpensive*

Shanghai 456
Hotel Lisboa,
Avenida da Amizade
Tel: 388404, 388474
Regarded by some as the best Shanghainese restaurant in both Macau and Hong Kong. The menu includes fried prawns with chilli sauce, chicken in shark's fin soup, fried yellow fish with sweet and sour sauce and Peking duck. Open 11–1am. *Moderate*

Restaurante Portugues dishes up home-style food

Tam Chai Yu Chun
Largo Governador
Tamagnini Barbosa,
Taipa Village
Tel: 327097
This traditional Cantonese restaurant is built into the side of a small Buddhist temple in the middle of Taipa village. Open 11am–11pm.
Inexpensive

Japanese

Furusato Nippon
Hotel Lisboa,
Avenida da Amizade
Tel: 388568
All the usual Japanese favourites – sushi, sashimi, tempuras etc – but at inflated Tokyo prices. Open 11–1am.
Expensive

Korean

Korean
Hotel Presidente,
Avenida da Amizade
Tel: 569039, 553888
Kimchi and grilled meats in an informal atmosphere. Open noon–3pm, 6pm–midnight. *Inexpensive*

Thai

Thai
27e Rua Abreu Nunes
Tel: 573288, 552255
This is the place to go if you get hungry at 4am. Probably the best Thai food in Macau. After all, this is where many of the Thai massage girls eat. Open noon– 6am. *Inexpensive*

Italian

Leung Un
46 Rua do Cunha,
Taipa Village
Tel: 327387
Locals call this the best Italian food in Macau. The menu includes pasta, salads, meat and fish. Open 11am–11pm. *Inexpensive*

International

A Pousada
Hyatt Regency Hotel, Taipa
Tel: 831234, ext 1861
Coffee-shop/cafe in a green-house setting with big windows that look onto the Hyatts lush gardens. A comprehensive menu of Asian and Western food. The daily lunch buffet is probably the best in Macau. Open 7am–midnight. *Inexpensive*

Noite E Dia
Hotel Lisboa,
Avenida da Amizade
Tel: 577666
A 24-hour cafe that serves punters taking a break from the action in the nearby casino. This is one of the few places in Macau where you can get an authentic Portuguese-style breakfast: scrambled eggs with spicy sausage, garlic bread and a hot cup of espresso. If you want to meet girls from the Crazy Paris show, this is the place to be as they often come here to eat.
Inexpensive

Safari
14 Patio do Cotovelo
Tel: 574313
Intimate and informal setting on a narrow lane off Avenida Almeida Ribeiro. The daily specials are a good bet. Open 9–1am.
Inexpensive

Nightlife

Macau's after dark scene has largely revolved around the casinos since gambling was legalized in 1964. Other late-night industries have sprung up to serve the casino clientele: bars and discotheques, strip shows, karaoke, hostess clubs and massage parlours.

Except for the Casino Victoria at the Jockey Club, all the gambling dens are open 24 hours daily. The only exception is during a number 8 typhoon warning, when only the Lisboa Casino continues to operate. The minimum bet is HK$20 and the official maximum is HK$60,000. Bets are placed in Hong Kong dollars, except at Kam Pek where patacas are accepted.

All casinos are operated under government franchise by the Sociadade de Turismo e Diversoes de Macau (STDM) which ensures the standardisation of all gambling rules. Gamblers must be at least 18 years old and photography in casinos is strictly prohibited. Winners are not obliged to tip as croupiers usually deduct about 10 percent of the winnings.

The most popular form of gambling are the 'hungry tigers' (slot machines), which take Ptc 1 or HK$1 coins. Blackjack is found at every casino (minumum bets range from HK$20–HK$100), but roulette is found only at the Lisboa these days. High rollers usually head for the baccarat tables, where the minimum bet is from HK$50–HK$1,000.

Macau also features a number of interesting Chinese gambling games.

Dai siu (big and small) centres around three dice thrown beneath a covered glass cannis-

Watch out for the 'Hungry Tigers'

Macau's nightlife revolves around casinos like this

ter. Bets are placed on the overall total or on whether the total sum of the dice will be of big or small value. If all three dice are the same number, the house takes all, except for bets on three of a kind. (Minimum bet: HK$5; highest table payout: HK$4,000.)

Fantan is a very old Chinese game in which the croupier plunges an inverted cup over a pile of numbered buttons and then slides the cup to one side. Once all the bets are in, the cup is lifted and the buttons are divided into groups of four until only one, two, three or four buttons remain. Winners are determined by the remaining numbers: odd or even, corners or divisions between numbers. (Minimum bet: HK$20; highest payout: HK$3,000.)

There is also no shortage of nightclubs and discos in Macau. Cover charges are from Ptc 60–150 which may include a complementary drink. Dress codes are generally lax at most nightspots and people in shorts, T-shirts and sandals are usually allowed in. Nightspots in hotels may have a more formal dress code.

Apart from casinos, hostess clubs, massage parlours, discos and night clubs, there is also a more refined side to the city's nightlife. The Macau Arts Festival takes place over a two-week period each spring, from mid-February to mid-March. Organized by the Instituto Cultural de Macau, the eclectic bill of fare includes Western and Chinese opera, folk dancing, marionettes, rock concerts, ballet, photo exhibitions and art shows.

The other highlight of the social calendar is the Macau International Music Festival each autumn, which draws socialites from Hong Kong and as far away as Portugal. The festival leans heavily towards European opera, chamber music and classical symphony. Venues include the Leal Senado Council Room, Monte Fort, Lou Lim Iok Gardens, the Forum, the church at St Joseph's Seminary and the University of Macau.

For information on either festival call 550902 or 343972.

Casinos

(Open 24 hours)

Hyatt Regency
Taipa
Tel: 831234
The hotel's Taipa Casino features blackjack, baccarat and *dai siu*.

Jai Alai
Jai Alai Building
Avenida da Amizade
Tel: 726129
Located in the old *jai alai* arena, the casino features blackjack, baccarat, slots and popular Chinese games like *fantan*, *dai siu* and *pai kao*.

Kam Pek
Avenida Almeida Ribeiro
Tel: 562654
An older casino, frequented mostly by local Chinese. Games include blackjack, baccarat, slots, *fantan* and *dai siu*. This is the only casino where patacas are accepted; all other casinos use Hong Kong dollars.

Lisboa
Avenida da Amizade
Tel: 577666, 377666
Blackjack, baccarat, slot machines, roulette, *dai siu*, *fantan*, and *pai kao*.

Macau Palace (Floating Casino)
Rua das Lorcas
Tel: 346702
Blackjack, baccarat, slots, *fantan*, *dai siu* and *pai kao*.

Victoria
Macau Jockey Club, Taipa
Tel: 321888
Weekends and mid-week race days only, 11am–3pm. Blackjack, baccarat, slots and *dai siu*.

Bars, Nightclubs & Discos

The Bar
Hyatt Regency, Taipa
Tel: 831234
The Bar (daily noon–2am) serves two drinks for the price of one during happy hour (5pm–7pm). Darts competition on Thursday (from 5pm). A jazz trio called The Bridge plays on Friday (10pm–1am).

Bar da Guia
Mandarin Oriental Hotel
Avenida da Amizade
Tel: 587888
Elegant bar (daily 5.30pm–2am) with a waterfront setting. Live entertainment (Tuesday–Sunday) provided by a talented Filipino house band.

Naughty night out at the Crazy Paris show

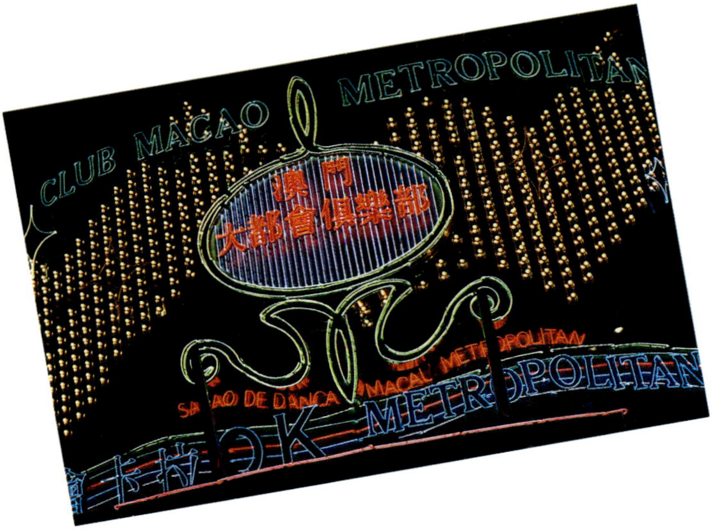

Mondial Disco
Hotel Mondial
8–10 Rua da Antonio Basto
Tel: 566866
Locals consider this the best pure disco in town. Packed to the rafters on Friday and Saturday nights (10pm–4am) with local revellers, especially young Portuguese. Music reflects the current dance charts in Europe and America. Cover charge: Ptc 80 plus tax and service charge, includes two drinks.

Portas Do Sol
Hotel Lisboa
Avenida da Amizade
Tel: 577666, 377666
Portas do Sol is for the older generation of Portuguese expats; couples who prefer Glen Miller to Metallica. Open 7pm–1am for dinner dancing.

Strip Shows

Crazy Paris
Hotel Lisboa
Avenida da Amizade
Tel: 577666, 377666
After running for more than 14 years, Crazy Paris is a Macau institution, soft porn disguised as a musical revue. The girls take it all off – but only for a fraction of a second at the end of each routine. No drinks, no food, no photos – all you do is watch. Tickets are Ptc 170. Shows at 8pm and 9.30pm nightly; an extra show on Saturday at 11pm. No admittance for under-18s.

Skylight
President Hotel
Avenida da Amizade
Tel: 553888
Skylight is described as part-disco, part-supper club and part-cabaret. The floorshow each evening is a striptease by European 'artists' in glitzy costumes. The club has glass walls and ceilings to allow guests a view of the night sky and harbour. Cover charge: Ptc 48, includes one drink. Open 9pm–4am.

Karaoke

Metropolitan
New Century Hotel, Taipa
Tel: 831111
Apart from a nightclub with a Filipino band and risque floorshow, the club (open 8pm–4am) offers two sets of karaoke lounges – one for men 'out on the town' and a 'wholesome' section for families.

Hostess club beckons

MOULIN ROUGE
New World Emperor Hotel
Rua de Xangai
Tel: 781888, 782287
One of the newer karaoke lounges. Open 8pm–4am.

Hostess Clubs

CHINA CITY
Jai Alai Building
Avenida da Amizade
Tel: 312333
As opulent as its sister club in Hong Kong, China City is for those who desire an evening of companionship with pretty Asian women. The company of a hostess will cost you Ptc 30 per 12 minutes with a minimum charge of Ptc 200. A live band and DJ provide the background music. Little English is spoken. Open 6pm–4am.

CLUB DE SAVOY
Hotel Lisboa
Avenida da Amizade
Tel: 332222
A relatively new club, the luxurious Savoy offers 100 Asian hostesses, a live band and karaoke rooms. Open 6pm–4am.

TONNOCHY
Si Toi Building
Rua da Praia Grande
Tel: 303538
Situated in a downtown office building, the Tonnochy boasts 180 beautiful girls plus live music and private karaoke rooms. Ptc 200 minimum charge. Open 6pm–4am.

Sauna and Massage

Located all over town, they are open from noon to around 5am. Standards, prices and services vary widely. The venues are primarily staffed by Filipino and Thai women.

CENTRO SAUNA MASSAGE TIN VONG
72 Avenida Ferreira de Almeida
Tel: 593553

DARLING THAI MASSAGE AND SAUNA
Jai Alai Building
Avenida da Amizade
Tel: 337733

SAUNA MONA LISA
Si Toi Building
Rua da Praia Grande
Tel: 565888

LISBOA HEALTH SPA
Hotel Lisboa
Avenida da Amizade

Tel: 593888 (men), 345333 (women)
No funny business here – this is legitimate sauna and massage. Separate sections for males (1pm–7am) and females (9am–7am). Open all night.

Performing Arts

The Forum
Avenida do Dr Rodrigo Rodrigues
Tel: 568711
Premier venue for big concerts, indoor sporting events and cultural shows. The arena hosts a big Chinese

New Year Musical Show each year, as well as Chinese opera.

Teatro Dom Pedro V
Largo Santo Agostinho
Currently undergoing renovation, the Dom Pedro hosts events of the music and arts festivals, as well as independent music, dance and drama.

Teatro No Complexo Escolar
Rua Luis Goncaga Gomes
Tel: 700751
The School Complex Theatre hosts music, dance and drama on a regular basis, especially performances by various school troupes under the Department of Education.

Folk Music

Macanese Evening
Pousada de Mongha
Tel: 561252
Mongha Fort is the dramatic location for a Macanese evening, every Friday from 7–9.30pm. Hosted by the Macau Tourism School, there is a buffet with local specialities and traditional Portuguese folk music from the Tuna Macanese Band. (Cost: Ptc 95 for adults; Ptc 50 for children). Reservations must be made 24 hours in advance.

Cinemas

The following cinemas show English-language films on a regular basis:

Teatro Capitol
Rua Sao Domingos

Estudio 3
Rua Santa Clara
(next to St Francis Garden)

Calendar of Special Events

Macau might just have more annual holidays and festivals then any other place on earth, with both Portuguese Catholic feast days and traditional Chinese celebrations. As a result, there is a special event nearly every week. Public holidays are marked with an asterisk in the list below. As the dates and celebrations of some events vary, please check with the Macau Government Tourist Office (Main office: No 9 Largo do Senado, Tel: 315566, Fax: 510104; daily 9am–6pm).

JANUARY–FEBRUARY

Lunar New Year*: The most important holiday for local Chinese, a joyous time when many of Macau's homes and offices are decorated with colourful lights and banners, flower bouquets and kumquat trees. A big family feast is held on New Year's Eve, but the following morning is reserved for solemn prayer at the local Buddhist temple.

MARCH–APRIL

Feast of Our Lord of Passion (Nosso Senhor dos Passos): Macau's most important Roman Catholic celebration, falling on the first weekend of Lent. The ritual starts with a Saturday evening procession from St Augustine's Church to Macau Cathedral where an all-night vigil ensues. The following day, a large crowd gathers as a statue of Christ is carried through the streets of Macau on a solemn march past each station of the cross to St Augustine's.

Ching Ming*: Buddhist devotees flock to cemeteries to clean the graves of their honourable ancestors, followed by a family picnic.

Chinese New Year decorations

The Procession of Our Lord of Passos

Easter Weekend*: A long and pious affair, with the public holiday stretching from Good Friday to Easter Monday. Every church in town is packed, but the main celebrations are held within the stout 19th century walls of the Macau Cathedral.

MAY–JUNE

Feast of Our Lady of Fatima (13 May): A date that is cherished by every Portuguese Catholic, celebrating the day in 1917 when the Blessed Virgin appeared before a farm girl at Fatima, Portugal. In Macau, the holiday is marked by a sombre procession between St Dominic's and Penha churches. There is also a special Mass at Our Lady of Fatima Church at Rua de Lei Pou Chon.

A-Ma Festival: This is the Macau equivalent of the boisterous Tin Hau Festival in Hong Kong, when local fishermen give thanks to Tin Hau, Goddess of the Sea and protector of sailors. Catch the colourful celebrations at A-Ma Temple and don't miss the gaily-decorated fishing craft on display at the inner harbour. The festival takes place on the 23rd day of the third lunar month.

Dragon Boat Festival*: This festival honours a high-minded government official who drowned himself in protest against official corruption. Fearing that his body would be eaten by fish, his sympathizers rowed out to the sea beating drums and throwing rice dumplings into the water to distract the fish. Spectators crowd along the waterfront at the Inner Harbour to cheer their favourite teams to victory. Teams from Asia and North America compete in various categories.

Feast of St Anthony of Lisbon (13 June): A ceremony is held at St Anthony's Church, during which the President of the Macau Senate presents 'wages' to the saint for protecting the colony the preceding year.

Feast of St John the Baptist* (24 June): St John the Baptist is the patron of the Portuguese colony, but only by accident. On June 24th, 1622 Portuguese priests and slaves defeated a Dutch invasion force with a 'lucky' cannon shot they attributed to St John's divine intervention.

Feast of Kwan Tai*: Buddhist holy day honouring Kwan Tai, an ancient Chinese soldier and scholar who became a god in the after-life. He has

Mid-Autumn Festival

an eclectic heavenly portfolio that includes war, literature, riches and pawnshops. Kwan Tai is also worshipped by cops and robbers, and many of the police stations in Macau bear a small Kwan Tai shrine. The festival falls on the 24th day of the sixth lunar month.

JULY–AUGUST

Battle of July 13th: Celebrated only in Taipa and Coloane, this holiday celebrates a fierce 1910 battle during which the Portuguese rid the islands of the last of the Pearl River pirates.
Festival of the Hungry Ghosts: Buddhist devotees burn paper offerings in front of homes and shops to ward off the restless spirits said to inhabit the earth in late summer.

SEPTEMBER–OCTOBER

Mid-Autumn (Lantern) Festival*: The Chinese version of the Harvest Festival, a magical evening that is illuminated by paper lanterns hung in homes, temples and restaurants.
Cheung Yeung Festival: Another time for cleaning the graves of one's departed ancestors.

NOVEMBER–DECEMBER

Macau Grand Prix (late November): Not just one race, but a series of gruelling chases through the bare streets of Macau, a thunderous weekend that features everything from fleet Formula Three cars to motorcycles and vintage cars.
Christmas Day and eve* (24–25 December): Try to catch Midnight Mass at a Catholic church to hear Christmas hymns in lilting Portuguese.

OTHER PUBLIC HOLIDAYS

New Year's Day (1 January)
Anniversary of the 1974 Portuguese Revolution (25 April)
Labour Day (1 May)
Camoes and Portugal Communities Day (10 June)
Portuguese Republic Day (5 October)
Portuguese Independence Day (1 December)
Feast of the Immaculate Conception (8 December)

Practical Information

GETTING THERE

By Sea

The most popular way to go to Macau is via ferry from Hong Kong. From Macau Ferry Terminal at Shun Tak Centre (200 Connaught Road, Western District, Hong Kong), you can take a jetfoil, jumbocat, hydrofoil, high-speed ferry, hovercraft or a steamer.

Jetfoils (7am–3am) offer the fastest (under an hour) and smoothest ride with a cruising speed of about 40 knots. Far East Jetfoil runs the 260-passenger Boeing service; there are first and ordinary classes and non-smoking sections on both levels. Upper deck fare is HK$126 on weekdays, HK$134 on weekends and public holidays, and HK$158 for night services. Fares on the lower deck are HK$119 on all days and HK$138 for night services.

Macau ferries

The Hong Kong Macau Hydrofoil Company (HMH) operates jumbocats (winter 7am–5pm; summer 9.30am–6pm) from Shun Tak Centre and China Ferry Terminal in Kowloon. The jet-propelled catamarans can carry about 300 passengers. Journey time: about 70 minutes. Weekdays: HK$118, weekends: HK$129. Night service is not available.

Sealink's hover-ferries run from 8.30am – late evening. Each hover-ferry carries about 250 passengers and completes the crossing in about an hour. Weekdays: HK$60, weekends: HK$73, night service: HK$86. This service operates only from China Ferry Terminal in Kowloon.

High-speed ferries run from 7.30am–10.15pm daily. Journey time: about 90 minutes. Comfortable vessels with sun decks and lounge. Weekdays: HK$52 (economy), HK$84 (first), weekends: HK$67 (economy), HK$96 (first). Snacks, videos and gambling on board.

Tickets can be bought at major travel agents and most hotels in Hong Kong or can be purchased up to 28 days in advance at Ticketmate outlets at Exchange Square and major MTR stations in Hong Kong. For more information, call the following Hong Kong numbers: Jetfoil (Tel: 8596596); hydrofoil and jumbocats (Tel: 5599255); hover ferries (Tel: 5423081); high-speed ferries (Tel: 8153043, 8032255).

By Air

Until the new international airport is completed in 1995, the only way to get to Macau by air is by the East Asia Airlines (EAA) helicopter service. Flights (9am–5.30pm) on eight-seater Bell 222 choppers which depart from the Macau

Helicopter services

Ferry Terminal, Hong Kong, and land at the Macau-Hong Kong Maritime Teminal in Macau 20 minutes later. Fares: HK$986 on weekdays, HK$1,086 on weekends. Credit cards not accepted. Baggage allowance: 5kg (11 lbs).

Bookings at Counter 8, 3rd floor, Shun Tak Centre (Tel: 8593359) or Macau Tourist Information Board, 3704 Shun Tak Centre (Tel: 5408180) in Hong Kong; Macau-Hong Kong Maritime Terminal (Tel: 572983, 550777) in Macau.

Departure Tax

The Hong Kong government charges ferry passengers HK$26, helicopter passengers HK$86. Macau charges Ptc 20 tax on all ferry departures, but the fee is included in all return tickets from Hong Kong.

TRAVEL ESSENTIALS

When To Visit

The best time to visit Macau is September–January when you can expect clear, sunny skies. From late December onwards, pack some winter clothes as it may be chilly. Expect rain and, possibly, thick fog from February–May. Summer can be hot and humid. Typhoon season is from May–September, so you may get stranded for a few days if the ferries are forced to stay in port.

Macau is extremely crowded on weekends and public holidays when regional gamblers descend on the Portuguese colony, and during the annual Macau Grand Prix in November.

Visas

All visitors to Macau must have a valid passport, except for Hong Kong Chinese who can enter with their identity cards.

Visas are not required for stays of up to six months for citizens of Portugal, Austria, Australia, Belgium, Brazil, Britain, Canada, Denmark, France, Germany, Greece, Italy, Japan, Malaysia, the Netherlands, New Zealand, Norway, the Philippines, Spain, Sweden, Switzerland, Thailand and the United States. Hong Kong residents are granted unlimited stay while British Commonwealth subjects are allowed a maximum 20-day stay without visa. Other nationalities are allowed a maximum of three days.

Visa are available at Portuguese embassies and consulates around the world. They cost HK$95 per person for tourist groups, HK$190 for individuals, and HK$380 for an entire family. Nationals of countries that do not maintain diplomatic relations with Portugal must obtain a visa before arrival.

Vaccinations

Not required.

Customs

No restrictions or duty on personal effects or money as long as the amount is reasonable. The exception is the import of drugs and firearms, which are prohibited without a licence.

However, until the new international airport is in operation, you should take note of Hong Kong's import restrictions: one bottle of wine, 200 cigarettes or 50 cigars or 250 grams of tobacco. Residents of Hong Kong are allowed less: one bottle of table or port wine, 100 cigarettes or 25 cigars.

Climate

The climate varies from moderate to hot, with an average annual temperature of just over 20°C (68°F). Humidity ranges from 73–90 percent. The annual rainfall is between 100–200cm (40–80 inches).

Macau has three distinct seasons. Spring

Hot and humid summers

Macau Skyline with Lisboa Hotel in foreground

is from February to May when you can expect wet, overcast and sometimes foggy weather. Daytime temperatures range from 17°C (63°F) in February to 28°C (82°F) in May. As summer approaches, the southwest monsoon brings moist, hot weather from equatorial Asia and the heat and humidity take over. From June to August, temperatures of 35°C (95°F) are not uncommon. There is also a good chance of thunderstorms and even a typhoon, or at least a typhoon warning during this time.

Macau cools down and dries off during the autumn/winter season, when the northeast monsoon takes over. From September to January you can expect clear and sunny skies, with temperatures between 13–29°C (55–84°F).

Clothing

Macau is still quite informal in a relaxed, Iberian sort of way. But you must dress appropriately for the seasons. In summer, shorts, T-shirts, sneakers and a bathing suit are all you need for daytime, a pair of slacks or a cotton dress for evening. Only the very best restaurants require a jacket and tie. Be warned: even at the height of summer, you may need a light jacket or sweater for the notoriously chilly air-conditioning in some hotels, restaurants and offices.

From November through April the temperature can vary dramatically, so it is best to pack both light and warm clothes. In general, dress in layers that can be peeled off or put back on according to temperature shifts. The height of winter can be quite cool; a heavy jacket is recommended just in case.

Electricity

Power outlets in Macau are mostly 220 volts, 50 cycles, but there are still 110 volts outlets in some older buildings.

Time

Macau is 8 hours ahead of GMT and 13 hours ahead of EST in the US. There is no daylight savings.

Business Hours

Government offices are open Monday–Friday 9am–5.30pm, with a siesta period between 1–3pm. Saturday hours are 9am–12.30pm. Banks are open Monday–Friday 9.30am–4pm and Saturday 9.30–noon.

Private companies are usually open Monday–Friday 9am–5.30 or 6pm, with siesta 1–3pm, and Saturday 9am–noon. Shops open 8.30–10am and close 8.30–9pm. Chain stores are usually open 11am–10pm. Shops are open all day Saturday, but close for lunch.

Photographic Supplies

Photo Princesa at 55-59 Avenida Infante D Henrique (Tel: 575959) has a wide range of slide and print film, plus cameras, lenses and accessories.

One-hour photo service is offered at Foto Nice, 57 Rua da Barra (Monday–Saturday 10am–10.30pm) and Photo Lily, 30A Rua da Praia Grande (Monday–Saturday 9.30am–8pm).

GETTING ACQUAINTED

Geography

Macau is located at latitude 21° 11' north and longitude 113° 33' east, on the southeast coast of China, on the southern shore of the Pearl River estuary. It is 60km (37¼ miles) west of Hong Kong.

The majority of the half million population live on the 6½-sq km (2½-sq mile) peninsula. The population of the two outlying islands – Taipa and Coloane – is much smaller but it is growing rapidly as the islands undergo development. A 2.4-km (1½-mile) bridge connects the mainland with Taipa (4.4sq km/1.7sq miles) and a 2.1-km (1.3-mile) causeway connects Taipa with Coloane (7.7sq km/3sq miles). A second bridge between the mainland and Taipa was completed in late 1993.

Government

Until the territory reverts to China on December 20, 1999, Macau is ruled by a Lisbon-appointed governor assisted by an Advisory Council and seven secretaries. There is also a legislative council comprising appointed and elected members.

Religion

Macau is a predominantly Buddhist country, with heavy Taoist and Confucian influences. Roman Catholics form a small but vocal minority, including ethnic Chinese, Macanese and Portuguese.

Taoist A-Ma temple

Population

Ethnic Chinese comprise the vast majority (95 percent) of the 400,000 population, with minorities of Portuguese (three percent) and Macanese or Eurasian residents (two percent). All the Chinese are Cantonese-speaking.

MONEY MATTERS

Currency

The official currency is the pataca. But Hong Kong dollars are widely circulated and accepted. At the time of publication, Ptc 103.3=HK$100 with a permissible variation of up to 10 percent. Most people trade at one to one. There are approximately eight patacas to US$1.

The pataca is divided into 100 avos. There are 5, 10, 50 100 and 500 pataca notes; 1 and 5 pataca coins; 10, 20 and 50 avos coins.

Major credit cards are accepted in hotels and larger restaurants. Travellers' cheques are also widely accepted. There is no restriction on the amount of money you bring in or take out of Macau.

Best exchange rates available at commercial banks (open Monday–Friday 9.30am–4pm, Saturday 9.30am–noon). You can also exchange money at your ho-

A Chinese-style bus stop

tel, casinos, official money changers or the exchange windows at the ferry terminal. There are no controls on money exchange in Macau.

Tipping

Most establishments add a 5 percent government 'tourism tax' and most hotels and restaurants add 10 percent service charge. It is customary for visitors to leave an additional 10–15 percent tip.

GETTING AROUND

Taxis

Taxis are cheap and plentiful. All are metred, with a Ptc 6.50 flag-down rate. After the first 1½km you will be charged 80 avos per 500m (546yds). There is a surcharge on journeys from the mainland to the outer islands, an additional Ptc 5 for Taipa and Ptc 10 for Coloane. No surcharge for return journeys.

Taxi stand next to the Ferry Terminal

A major drawback is the fact that most drivers are unlikely to know the English or Portuguese name for a given street or building – just the unofficial Chinese name. Ask the hotel staff to write down your destination in Chinese or carry a bilingual map. Cabbies do not expect a tip beyond rounding off to the nearest pataca. Tel: 519519 or 371035 for radio cabs.

Buses

Buses run from 7am–midnight and offer cheap transport for the more adventurous traveller, with fares ranging from Ptc 1.80–3.50. They can be overcrowded and a bit chaotic.

Route information at most bus stops is in Chinese and most drivers speak only Cantonese. Check with your hotel staff, tour operator or the staff of the Macau Government Tourist Office (MGTO) on fares and bus numbers before setting off.

Pedicabs

This is the Macau equivalent of the rickshaw – a tricycle that seats three people, including the driver. Although the drivers offer guided tours, their English is seldom good enough to give you any real information. But it's still fun to try the oldest (and slowest) means of transportation in Macau. If a driver refuses to take you somewhere, it's because many of the city's hills are too steep for pedicabs. Agree on a price before you set off. A good rule of thumb is Ptc 10 for a short ride or Ptc 50–60 for a one-hour sightseeing trip.

Bicycles

Assuming you are fit, bikes offer a practical means of transportation, especially in the old parts of town where the streets are narrow and the traffic quite bad at times, or in the outlying islands with their country roads. Bicycles are not allowed across the Macau-Taipa Bridge.

There are no bicycle rental shops on mainland Macau. On Taipa, the main square in the village is surrounded by them and there is another (Si Toi Shop, rate: Ptc 40 for five hours) next to Pak Tai Temple. Hyatt Regency also offers bikes to its guests. Bicycle rental rates are Ptc 10–12 per hour.

Mokes

Mokes are small, jeep-like vehicles, perfect for getting around the outer islands or the narrow cobblestoned streets of the old town. Cost: Ptc 320 per day on weekends, Ptc 280 per day on weekdays; deposit: Ptc 300; insurance coverage: Ptc 50. You must refill the gas tank before returning the Moke.

Drivers must be at least 21 years old and the holder of a recognised driving licence for a least two years. International licences are also accepted. Mokes come with detachable canvas roofs and plastic side panels; baby seats are available on request. For reservations, Tel: 378851 (Macau) or Tel: 5434190 (Hong Kong).

Car Rental

Both self-drive and chauffeur-driven cars are available in Macau. Expect to pay about Ptc 300 per day for self-drive; Ptc 100 an hour for chauffeur-driven. Most taxis can also be rented by the hour. The rate reflects your bargaining skills, but

try not to pay more than Ptc 80 an hour. Avis also hires out 1920s-style London buses at Ptc 250 per hour.

AVIS RENT-A-CAR
Tel: 336789, 555686, 567888 (Macau)
Tel: 5412011 (Hong Kong)

To/From the Ferry Terminal

Many hotels offer a free pick-up service from the ferry terminal if you let them know which boat you will be arriving on. Otherwise, grab a cab or rent a Moke. If you are staying on the mainland, and do not have too much luggage, you can hire a pedicab.

Maps

MGTO tourist offices offer a good selection of basic maps. If you want something more detailed, try the 'Universal Map of Macau & Zhuhai', with street names in English and Chinese characters. Available at bookstores in Hong Kong and Macau.

ACCOMMODATION

Thanks to gambling, Macau has a good number of hotels. But they tend toward the medium-range and luxury categories, with very little at the shoestring end. Hotels are especially crowded on weekends and public holidays when Hong Kong punters flood over, and during the Macau Grand Prix week in November.

An approximate guide to current room rates (standard double) is:
$=under US$30; $$=US$30–US$60; $$$=US$60–US$90; $$$$=over US$90.

BELA VISTA
8 Rua do Comendador Kou Ho Neng
Tel: 965333; Fax: 965588
The grand old dame of the South China coast has been transformed into one of

the top luxury hotels in Asia under the aegis of the Mandarin Oriental group. Most of the eight suites offer sweeping views of the Outer Harbour. Lunch on the terrace is a must. *$$$$*

Beverly Plaza
Avenida do Dr Rodrigo Rodrigues
Tel: 782288; 7396993 (Hong Kong)
Fax: 780684
Basic service at a moderate price for those who plan on spending most of their time away from the room. Good location near the Lisboa and downtown Macau. *$$$*

Cantao
62 Rua do Guimarae
off Avenida Almeida Ribeiro
Tel: 922416
A ramshackle old place near the Inner Harbour, wedged between two streets that look like they haven't changed in a hundred years. The Cantao does not offer much in the way of modern facilities, but it's hard to beat the old fashioned Asian atmosphere. *$*

Central
26–28 Avenida Almeida Ribeiro
Tel: 373309
True to its name, the budget Central is right in the heart of the action, a block west of Largo do Senado and right next to St Dominic's Market. Facilities are basic but cheap. *$*

Hyatt Regency
2 Estrada Almirante Marques Esparteiro
Taipa
Tel: 831234; 5590168 (Hong Kong)
Fax: 830195
The Hyatt Regency offers luxury service in a resort atmosphere on Taipa Island. The grounds feature a huge tropical garden, free-form swimming pool and tennis courts. The restaurants and bars are among the best in Macau, and the staff is very friendly. *$$$$*

Lisboa
Avenida da Amizade
Tel: 577666; 8593333 (Hong Kong)
Fax: 567193
The Lisboa is the only place in Macau that comes close to matching the fascinating gaudiness of a Vegas hotel. The outside looks like a cross between a Chinese

Lisboa Hotel

temple and the Starship Enterprise, while the public areas and guest rooms offer a nostalgic glimpse of the psychedelic 1960s. But you can't beat the location: right in the middle of town. *$$$*

LONDON
4–6 Praca Ponte e Horta
Tel: 937761, 83388
Tucked away on a quiet square off Rua das Lorchas, the London overlooks the Inner Harbour and is within walking distance of the old town. Good value for your money. *$*

MANDARIN ORIENTAL
Avenida da Amizade
Tel: 567888; 8811988 (Hong Kong)
Fax: 594589
This elegant waterfront hotel is still one of the better places to stay in Macau. It has impeccable service and luxurious decor, and conveniently located next to the ferry terminal. *$$$$*

Mandarin Oriental

MATSUYA
5 Calcada de Sao Francisco
Tel: 575466; 3686181 (Hong Kong)
Fax: 575466
The Matsuya is a bit worn, but the location at the base of Guia Lighthouse affords panoramic views of the harbour. *$$*

METROPOLE
63 Rua da Praia Grande
Tel: 388166; Fax: 330890
Catering mainly to Chinese visitors, the Metropole is located in the heart of downtown Macau, within walking distance of the Lisboa Casino and the old town. *$$*

POUSADA DE COLOANE
Cheoc Van Beach, Coloane
Tel: 328144, 328143;
5455626 (Hong Kong)
Overlooking Cheoc Van Beach, this pousada has been a favourite with Hong Kong expats for many years. The rooms are somewhat rundown, but Coloane does have a certain tacky charm. *$$*

Pousada De Coloane

POUSADA DE SAO TIAGO
Avenida da Republica
Tel: 378111, 739 1216; 7353368 (Hong Kong); Fax: 552170
Some people think this is the most romantic place to stay in the entire Orient. Sao Tiago is set within the ruins of Barra Fort at the tip of the Macau Peninsula, overlooking the Inner Harbour's entrance. The Iberian ambience is accentuated by great stone facades and banyan trees all around. *$$$$*

PRESIDENTE
69 Avenida Da Amizade
Tel: 553888; 8571533 (Hong Kong)
Fax: 552735
Right on the waterfront, the 333-room Presidente offers marvellous harbour views and quick access to the casinos along Avenida Amizade. *$$$*

ROYAL
2–4 Estrada da Vitoria
Tel: 552222; 5486333 (Hong Kong)
Fax: 563008
The Royal is operated by the Dai-Ichi group, which makes it the top Japanese-style hotel in Macau. Overlooking Vasco da Gama Square, the location of this ho-

tel offers quick access to downtown Macau and the old town. *$$$$*

Sintra
58–62 Avenida D Joao IV
Tel: 710111; 5408028 (Hong Kong)
Fax: 510527
As an old standby, the Sintra has seen better days. But it still offers good value for money and a great location near the Lisboa and Praia Grande. *$$*

Westin Resort
Hac Sa Beach, Coloane
Tel: 871111; 8032015 (Hong Kong)
Fax: 871122
The new Westin offers something that no other hotel in town can match: an 18-hole golf course. And that alone will keep it full for years to come. The black sands of Hac Sa Beach are just outside the front door, and there are grass tennis courts around the back. A casino is on the cards for the future. *$$$$*

White Swan Hotel
Shamian Island
Guangzhou
China
Tel: 8886968, Telex: 44688 WSH CN
Hong Kong reservations office:
504 Pedder Building
12 Pedder Street
Tel: 5240192/ 3
A five-star hotel that towers 22-storeys over Shamian Island, with half the rooms looking onto the Pearl River and the other half overlooking the old European mansions and churches of Shamian. The lobby is a feast of modern Chinese eccentricity with fish ponds, pavilions and a waterfall. There are arts and crafts shops in its basement and the hotel boasts some of the best restaurants in southern China. *$$$*

HEALTH & EMERGENCIES

Hygiene/General Health

Conditions are similar to Hong Kong. Water is safe to drink in the five-star hotels; otherwise, stick to bottled or mineral water. If you don't live in Asia, you should be careful with street food because it probably contains different strains of bacteria from what you are used to in your country.

Emergency: Dial 999 (for the police, fire station or ambulance service).

Hospitals

Macau has modern clinics and hospitals with the latest high-tech equipment and staffed with doctors from medical schools in Europe and North America.

The following hospitals have 24-hour emergency rooms:

Centro Hospitalar
Estrada Visconde de Sao Januario
Tel: 577199

The Iberian-inspired Westin Resort

Hospitalar Kiang Vu
Estrada do Repouso
Tel: 378311

Night Pharmacies

Night pharmacies operate 9pm–9am.
Sunday: Farmacia Tsan Heng, 7 Avenida Almeida Ribeiro.
Monday, Tuesday and Thursday: Farmacia Lap Kei, 3D Calcada do Guia.
Thursday and Friday: Farmacia Popular, 16 Largo do Senado.
Saturday: Farmacia Uniao, 17 Rua Ferreira do Amaral.

Crime/ Trouble

Macau is relatively crime-free, but as is the case elsewhere in the world, it is not a good idea to carry large amounts of cash or expensive jewellery around the city streets. Muggings do happen, but there is very little violent crime in Macau, compared with most large American and European cities.

COMMUNICATIONS & NEWS

Post & Telephone

The General Post Office is located at the corner of Largo do Senado and Avenida Almeida Ribeiro. The philately desk sells stamps from Macau, Portugal, Madeira and the Azores. Open Monday–Saturday 8am–midnight, Sunday and public holidays 9am–midnight.

Most hotels offer International Direct Dial (IDD) telephone services from the rooms. You can also make IDD calls from the GPO and its branches on Taipa and Coloane. If using an AT&T phone card, dial access number: 0800-111. Public telephone booths are blue and yellow. A one-pataca coin will get you five minutes of talk.

Useful Telephone Numbers:
Directory Inquiries: 181 (English & Chinese); 185 (Portuguese).
International Information: 101.
Time: 140 (English); 141 (Chinese); 145 (Portuguese).
Weather Forecasts: 911 (Portuguese); 912 (Chinese).

Courier

Urgent letters and packages can be sent by international courier.

DHL
14–16 Beco da Praia Grande
Edificio Hoi Tin
Tel: 569916; Fax: 338244

Federal Express
Avenida da Amizade
Tel: 703333

Media

Hong Kong's daily *South China Morning Post* (SCMP) is the most widely distributed English language newspaper in Macau. The *Hong Kong Standard*, *International Herald Tribune* and *Asian Wall Street Journal* are also available. Newspapers published in Macau include *Macau Hoje*, *Jornal de Macau*, *Comercia de Macau* and *Tribuna de Macau.*

Television & Radio

Macau has two local television station: TDM Canal 1 which broadcasts in Por-

Mini post office

tuguese, and TDM Canal 2 which broadcasts in Cantonese. However, Macau also receives three mainland China stations and Hong Kong's ATV and TVB's English and Cantonese broadcasts. If you want to sample the local airwaves, try Radio Vila Verde.

Language

Portuguese is the official language of Macau, but its use is generally restricted to government departments and street names. As 95 percent of the population is Chinese, the language of the streets is Cantonese. Most people in the tourism business speak passable English.

SPORTS & RECREATION

Beaches

If you want to spend a relaxing day at the beach, head for Taipa or Coloane where there are several good strands. The best known are on Coloane: Cheoc Van and Hac Sa beaches.

Flying

Experience Macau from a completely different perspective – the open cockpit of an Ultralite plane, which is basically a bicycle with wings. But be forewarned: this is not for the faint-hearted. A 10-minute flight costs Ptc 300. No reservations necessary, just arrive at the field on Avenida da Amizade opposite the Hotel Presidente. Open 10am–sunset. Tel: 782216; Fax: 782219.

If you get hooked after the first flight, you can learn how to pilot an Ultralite yourself. But first you have to join the Macau Aeronautical Association for Ptc 1,000, plus a one-year membership fee of

Ptc 1,000, Ptc 2,000 insurance, Ptc 23,000 instruction fee and Ptc 900 per hour for use of the aircraft.

Golf

The new Macau Golf and Country Club is next to the Westin Resort on Coloane Island. The 18-hole, par 71 course was designed according to championship standards, but it is only open to club members and Westin guests. The clubhouse offers swimming pool, tennis courts, sauna, steambath, jacuzzi, restaurants and bars. For more information call the Westin Resort (Tel: 871111) and the country club sales office in Hong Kong (Tel:

8032002, 5411812). Alternatively, head for the links at Zhongshan Hot Springs and Zhuhai across the border.

Greyhound Racing

The dogs race at the Canidrome on Avenida General Castelo Branco in northern Macau. (Tel: 574413; entrance fee: Ptc 5, minimum bet: Ptc 5.) The 10,000-seat track features computerized betting counters and a giant matrix screen which displays the odds.

Races are held from 8pm on Tuesday, Thursday, Saturday and Sunday, and public holidays. There are 14 races in a meet. If you do not want to go down to the Canidrome, off-track betting is available at the Lisboa and Kam Pek casinos, where the races are shown on closed-circuit television.

Horse Racing

The Macau Jockey Club is on the south shore of Taipa Island, close to the Hyatt Regency Hotel (Tel: 321888 in Macau or 5170872 in Hong Kong). Races are on grass or sand with horses imported from Australia, New Zealand and Britain. The track features an enclosed grandstand which seats 18,000 and has some of the most sophisticated betting equipment available, as well as a huge video matrix screen which displays odds, results and a close-up view of the races. (Entrance fee: Ptc 20, minimum bet: Ptc 10.) Races are staged nearly every Sunday afternoon; Saturday afternoon and Wednesday night meets are held about twice a month.

Horseback Riding

The Macau Horse Riding Centre at Hac Sa Beach has a stable full of gentle mounts for rides along the beach or on trails winding over the wooded hills of Coloane. Many of the horses are retired thoroughbreds from the Macau Jockey Club. The owner accompanies every outing. (Tel: 328302; hourly rate: Tuesday–Friday Ptc 250, weekends Ptc 300.) Helmets and boots included. Picnic lunches arrangeable on request.

Ice Skating

The Future Bright Amusement Park rink (Tel: 9892318; weekdays: Ptc 25 per hour, weekends: Ptc 35 per hour) is large enough to host international skating events. The skating school has five instructors including a former member of Holiday on Ice. The complex also houses a bowling alley, children's playground and food court. Future Bright is located on Praca de Luis de Camoes.

Motor Sports

The annual Macau Grand Prix is a two-day affair along a 6.1 km (3.8 mile) road circuit though the streets of Macau. The start/finish line, grandstand and pits are directly opposite the Mandarin Oriental

Hotel in Avenida da Amizade.

First-class drivers from around the world participate in Formula Three and production car races, as well as the motorbike event. There are also vintage car rallies. With crowds of 35,000 or more, the city is extremely crowded over Grand Prix week, so if you are not a motor sports fan, it may be wise to avoid Macau at this time.

For those who want to drive themselves, go-cart racing is available at a track on Taipa Island, adjacent to the Macau Jockey Club.

Running

Macau is well-supplied with jogging spots. A 1.7-km (1-mile) trail loops around the top of Colina da Guia, starting from the parking lot below the lighthouse or the upper part of Flora Gardens. A 8.6-km (5-mile) path leads around Alto Coloane mountain. And there is a 6.2-km (4-mile) trail between the helipad and Ka Ho village on the north side of Coloane. The Hyatt Regency Hotel on Taipa Island offers a jogging, walking and cycling map of three trails around Taipa and Coloane.

Other top jogging spots include Camoes Gardens, Montanha Russa Garden, Flora Garden, the Praia Grande waterfront between the Bank of China Building and Pousada de Sao Tiago, and the figure-eight loop around the top of Colina da Penha and Barra Hill.

Each December, about 1,000 runners compete in the Macau Marathon, which circles the mainland and two outer islands. There is a shorter, wheelchair race on the same day.

Sports Complex

The 4,000-seat Forum arena on Avenida do Dr Rodrigo Rodrigues offers indoor facilities for basketball, gymnastics, table tennis and volleyball.

Tennis & Squash

There are tennis and squash courts at the Hyatt Regency, Mandarin Oriental, New Century and Westin Resort hotels. The Hyatt offers the services of a professional tennis coach.

Water Sports

Windsurfing, kayaking and sailing are available at Hac Sa and Cheoc Van beaches on Coloane. Equipment can be rented from kiosks at Hac Sa Beach, or the boat club at Cheoc Van.

USEFUL ADDRESSES

Tourist Information

The Macau Government Tourist Office (MGTO) offers a good selection of maps and brochures, as well as 16mm films and video cassettes about the territory. Free copies of its Macau Travel Talk are available at leading hotels. MGTO's main office is at 9 Largo do Senado (Tel: 315566, Fax: 510104). Information counters are at the Macau-Hong Kong Maritime Terminal (Tel: 555424), Guia Lighthouse (Tel: 569808) and Monte Fort (Tel: 307315). MGTO offices are open daily 9am–6pm.

In addition, there is a Macau Tourist Information Board (MTIB) (Tel: 5408180; weekdays 9am–5pm, Saturday 9am–1pm) at the ferry terminal in Hong Kong. There is also a Macau tourism desk (Tel: 7697970; 8am–10pm) just outside the arrival hall at the Hong Kong International Airport.

Macau Ring is a fully automated on-line tourist information and reservation system available in Hong Kong. Using a tone-dial phone, call 9220-3022 and an interactive voice-response system will guide you with information on Macau, or help you make hotel, ferry and tour reservations. However, you can only access the system by paying a HK$20 (US$2.50) membership fee, a slight drawback to one-time users.

FURTHER READING

Fiction

The Lusiads by Luis Vaz de Camoes. Penguin, London, 1952. Epic verse by Portugal's national poet, penned in the late 16th century.

City of Broken Promises by Austin Coates. Oxford University Press, Hong Kong, 1988. A rags-to-riches love story by the resident doyen of the Hong Kong English literary scene.

Manchu by Robert Elegant. McGraw-Hill, New York, 1980 and Penguin Books, London, 1981. Historical drama that revolves around a young, Jesuit-educated Englishman who makes a fortune as a 17th-century China trader based in Macau.

History

The English In China 1600–1843 by J B Eames. Curson, London, 1974. Riveting story of English trade and diplomacy along the China coast leading up to the founding of Hong Kong.

Macau by Cesar Guillen-Nunez. Oxford University Press, Hong Kong, 1984. Easy to read history of Macau.

Photo Books

Viva Macau! by Shann Davies and Brian Brazier. MacMillan, Hong Kong, 1980. A pictorial history of 400 years of Macanese history, with text by long-time Macau expert Shann Davies.

Chinnery: The Man and the Legend by Robin Hutcheon and Geoffrey Bonsall. South China Morning Post Books, Hong Kong, 1975. A look at the life of prominent Irish artist George Chinnery (1774–1852) who painted scenes of Macau in the early 19th century.

Travel

Insight Guide: Hong Kong. Apa Publications, Singapore 1993. Includes a section on Macau.

Odyssey Illustrated Guide to Macau by Shann Davies. Odyssey, Hong Kong, 1993. A comprehensive guide to nearly every landmark in Macau, with photos by Richard Dobson.

Thrilling Cities by Ian Fleming. Reprint Society, London, 1964. The father of Cold War yarns took time off from James Bond to pen a book on his travels to various cities, including Macau.

ACKNOWLEDGMENTS

Cover	**Adina Tonvy/Apa Photo**
Back Cover	**Alain Everard/Apa Photo**
Photography	**Joseph R Yogerst** *and*
Pages 29B, 30T, 36B, 37T, 69, 77B, 78, 81T, 81M, 86T	**M Leaf/Apa Photo HKG**
53, 62, 65B, 67, 73T, 73B, 84B, 86B	**Shek Sai Wah/Apa Photo HKG**
12, 14T, 63, 65T, 67, 68, 70, 75	**Macau Govt Tourist Office**
76, 88	**Chris Davis/Apa Photo HKG**
14B, 16	**Manfred Morgenstern**
52, 72	**Virginia Lee**
15	**Leo Haks Collection**
13	**Museu da Marinha, Belém**
38	**Pousada de Sao Tiago**
5	**Sylvain Grandadam**

Copy Editor	**Kwan Chooi Tow**
Desktop Operator	**Caroline Low**
Handwriting	**V. Barl**
Cover Design	**Klaus Geisler**
Cartography	**Lovell Johns Ltd**

Index

G

H

I

J, K

L

M

N, O

P

R

S

T

U, V

Y, Z

INSIGHT GUIDES

COLORSET NUMBERS

160 Alaska
155 Alsace
150 Amazon Wildlife
116 America, South
173 American Southwest
158A Amsterdam
260 Argentina
287 Asia, East
207 Asia, South
262 Asia, South East
194 Asian Wildlife, Southeast
167A Athens
272 Australia
263 Austria
188 Bahamas
206 Bali Baru
107 Baltic States
246A Bangkok
292 Barbados
219B Barcelona
187 Bay of Naples
234A Beijing
109 Belgium
135A Berlin
217 Bermuda
100A Boston
127 Brazil
178 Brittany
109A Brussels
144A Budapest
260A Buenos Aires
213 Burgundy
268A Cairo
247B Calcutta
275 California
180 California, Northern
161 California, Southern
237 Canada
162 Caribbean The Lesser Antilles
122 Catalonia (Costa Brava)
141 Channel Islands
184C Chicago
151 Chile
234 China
135E Cologne
119 Continental Europe
189 Corsica
281 Costa Rica
291 Cote d'Azur
165 Crete
184 Crossing America
226 Cyprus
114 Czechoslovakia
247A Delhi, Jaipur, Agra
238 Denmark
135B Dresden
142B Dublin
135F Düsseldorf
204 East African Wildlife
149 Eastern Europe,
118 Ecuador
148A Edinburgh
268 Egypt
123 Finland
209B Florence
243 Florida
154 France
135C Frankfurt
208 Gambia & Senegal
135 Germany
148B Glasgow
279 Gran Canaria
169 Great Barrier Reef
124 Great Britain
167 Greece
166 Greek Islands
135G Hamburg
240 Hawaii
193 Himalaya, Western
196 Hong Kong
144 Hungary
256 Iceland
247 India
212 India, South
128 Indian Wildlife
143 Indonesia
142 Ireland
252 Israel
236A Istanbul
209 Italy
213 Jamaica
278 Japan
266 Java
252A Jerusalem-Tel Aviv
203A Kathmandu
270 Kenya
300 Korea
202A Lisbon
258 Loire Valley
124A London
275A Los Angeles
201 Madeira
219A Madrid
145 Malaysia
157 Mallorca & Ibiza
117 Malta
272B Melbourne
285 Mexico
285A Mexico City
243A Miami
237B Montreal
235 Morocco
101A Moscow
135D Munich
211 Myanmar (Burma)
259 Namibia
269 Native America
203 Nepal
158 Netherlands
100 New England
184E New Orleans
184F New York City
133 New York State
293 New Zealand
265 Nile, The
120 Norway
124B Oxford
147 Pacific Northwest
205 Pakistan
154A Paris
249 Peru
184B Philadelphia
222 Philippines
115 Poland
202 Portugal
114A Prague
153 Provence
156 Puerto Rico
250 Rajasthan
177 Rhine
127A Rio de Janeiro
172 Rockies
209A Rome
101 Russia
275B San Francisco
130 Sardinia
148 Scotland
184D Seattle
261 Sicily
159 Singapore
257 South Africa
264 South Tyrol
219 Spain
220 Spain, Southern
105 Sri Lanka
101B St Petersburg
170 Sweden
232 Switzerland
272 Sydney
175 Taiwan
112 Tenerife
186 Texas
246 Thailand
278A Tokyo
139 Trinidad & Tobago
113 Tunisia
236 Turkey
171 Turkish Coast
210 Tuscany
174 Umbria
237A Vancouver
198 Venezuela
209C Venice
263A Vienna
255 Vietnam
267 Wales
184C Washington DC
183 Waterways of Europe
215 Yemen

You'll find the colorset number on the spine of each Insight Guide.

INSIGHT *POCKET* GUIDES

EXISTING & FORTHCOMING TITLES:

Aegean Islands
Algarve
Alsace
Athens
Bali
Bali Bird Walks
Bangkok
Barcelona
Bavaria
Berlin
Bhutan
Boston
Brittany
Brussels
Budapest & *Surroundings*
Canton
Chiang Mai
Costa Blanca
Costa Brava
Cote d'Azur
Crete
Denmark
Florence
Florida
Gran Canaria
Hawaii
Hong Kong
Ibiza
Ireland
Istanbul
Jakarta
Kathmandu *Bikes & Hikes*
Kenya
Kuala Lumpur
Lisbon
Loire Valley
London
Macau
Madrid
Malacca
Mallorca
Malta
Marbella/ *Costa del Sol*
Miami
Milan
Morocco
Moscow
Munich
Nepal
New Delhi
New York City
North California
Oslo/Bergen
Paris
Penang
Phuket
Prague
Provence
Rhodes
Rome
Sabah
San Francisco
Sardinia
Scotland
Seville/Grenada
Seychelles
Sikkim
Singapore
South California
Southeast England
Sri Lanka
St Petersburg
Sydney
Tenerife
Thailand
Tibet
Turkish Coast
Tuscany
Venice
Vienna
Yogyakarta
Yugoslavia's *Adriatic Coast*

United States: **Houghton Mifflin Company, Boston MA 02108**
Tel: (800) 2253362 Fax: (800) 4589501

Canada: **Thomas Allen & Son, 390 Steelcase Road East**
Markham, Ontario L3R 1G2
Tel: (416) 4759126 Fax: (416) 4756747

Great Britain: **GeoCenter UK, Hampshire RG22 4BJ**
Tel: (256) 817987 Fax: (256) 817988

Worldwide: **Höfer Communications Singapore 2262**
Tel: (65) 8612755 Fax: (65) 8616438

"I was first drawn to the Insight Guides by the excellent "Nepal" volume. I can think of no book which so effectively captures the essence of a country. Out of these pages leaped the Nepal I know – the captivating charm of a people and their culture. I've since discovered and enjoyed the entire Insight Guide Series. Each volume deals with a country or city in the same sensitive depth, which is nowhere more evident than in the superb photography."

Sir Edmund Hillary